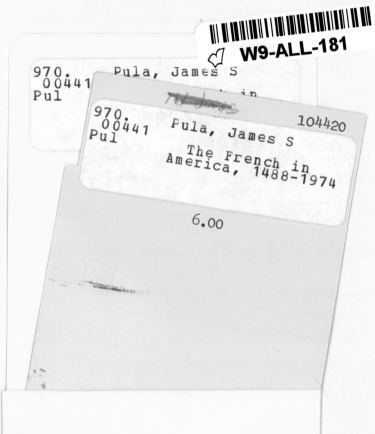

W9-ALL-181

970.
00441
Pul

Pula, James S

970.
00441
Pul

Pula, James S       104420

The French in
America, 1488-1974

6.00

ETHNIC CHRONOLOGY SERIES
NUMBER 20

# The French in America
# 1488-1974

## A Chronology & Fact Book

Compiled and edited by

## James S. Pula

1975
OCEANA PUBLICATIONS, INC.
DOBBS FERRY, NEW YORK

Library of Congress Cataloging in Publication Data
Main entry under title:

The French in America, 1488-1974.

(Ethnic chronology series; no. 20)
Bibliography: p.
Includes index.
1. French Americans--Chronology. 2. French-
Canadians--Chronology. 3. France--Relations (General)
with the United States. 4. United States--Relations
(General) with France. I. Pula, James S., 1946-
II. Series.
E184. F8F74        970'. 004'41        75-14292
ISBN 0-379-00515-8

970.00441
Pul

Manufactured in the United States of America

# TABLE OF CONTENTS

104420

## EDITOR'S FOREWORD

This book is dedicated to "Amos" and Napoleon (Beaseau) Smith, Lavinia du Pan, Alexis Nicol and Henriette Gendreau, sons and daughters of France who came to America to work in the logging camps of northern New York. Without their fortitude and perseverance my wife and I would not be here.

One has only to look at a map of the United States to perceive the far-ranging corners of the country to which French explorers and settlers ventured. Names like Prairie du Chien, Racine, Eau Claire, Terre Haute, Vincennes, Des Moines and Dubuque ring out a melodic song of France. Open a cookbook and see what you find: omelette, mousse, au gratin, hors d'oeuvres, crêpes suzette and julienne. Think of the games Americans play: croquet, poker, roulette and craps. Try to live for a day without uttering words like automobile, garage, lingerie, restaurant, crayon, bouquet or boutique, all bearing the unmistakable mark of the fleur-de-lis. French influence in American life is pervasive and obvious; but trying to discover who left these cultural footprints is another question.

A major problem that any researcher has in working with French immigration in the United States is uncovering geneologies buried beneath an avalanche of time and ethnic indifference. The French in the United States all too often obliterated their own trails completely. Place names and linguistic quirks remain as a lasting testimony to the influence of France on American culture, but the people have all but disappeared into an abyss of assimilation. Unlike many other national groups, the French generally held no special reluctance toward Anglicizing their names and their speech. Indeed, many did so automatically as a matter of course. In this way "Nicol" became "Nichols," "Le Blanc" transformed itself into "White," the "Letellier" family answered to "Taylor," "King" became the new moniker of "Le Roy," and "Le Brun" evolved into "Brown." While a Lafayette, a Chevalier, or a Cartier may protrude noticeably above the melting pot of Anglo-America, all too many descendants of Orléans, Brittany or Compaigne lie forever submerged beneath the enshrouding character of American culture.

In preparing this brief introduction to French influences on American life the intention has been to focus on the United States and not on French Canada. While the development of the two are inextricably linked, especially in the early centuries, this book in no way pretends to cover French influences in Canada. An attempt has been made to cover a broad range of topics, including entries from the fields of politics, military affairs, education, economics, science, sports, art, music, literature, and the cinema.

Naturally, this volume is the sum total of contributions made by a great many individuals. I would like to thank particularly Dr. William E. Gibbs, who lent his aid and assistance, and Cheryl Pula who typed part of the completed manuscript. Credit goes, as well, to the following individuals and institutions who provided me with substantial aid and assistance: Ms. Louise Courcy of the Union Saint-Jean-Baptiste; Ms. Martha M. Hermann of the French Azilum, Towanda, Pennsylvania; Mr. Jean-Pierre Guerin, Attaché Culturel de l'Ambassade de France (New York); Mr. Gilles Proulx, Archiviste Historien, Fortress of Louisbourg National Historical Park, Nova Scotia; and to the libraries at the State Historical Society of Wisconsin, the University of South Carolina, and Harvard University.

Finally, but by no means least, I want to thank my wife, Marilyn, who not only put up with the constant annoyance of a living room buried under 3x5 cards, but actually did much of the more laborious research that made this book possible.

James S. Pula
New York Mills, New York

1488    Some French historians maintain that a Dieppe navigator named Cousin, sailing off the west coast of Africa, was forced westward by a storm until he made a landfall off South America. A sailor on the voyage named Pinzon is said to have migrated to Spain where he later accompanied Christopher Columbus on his historical voyage to the New World.

1493    Pope Alexander VI divided the New World between Spain and Portugal. This later led to much bitterness between Spanish and French explorers in North America.

1500    By the beginning of the sixteenth century fishermen from all of the French ports between Dieppe and Bordeaux were regularly journeying to the area of the Grand Banks off Newfoundland, where they caught and cured cod and other fish products.

1504    Existing historical records show that numerous Norman, Breton, and Basque fishermen visited the Newfoundland cod banks. Their records seem to indicate that they had done so before Cabot's celebrated voyage of 1497.

        Easter Day. A giant wooden cross was erected in modern Canada by French sailors from the ship Espoir. The cross was engraved with the name of the Pope, King Louis XII, Admiral de Graville, and the crewmen.

1506    Jean Denys of Honfleur explored the North American coast in the vicinity of the Gulf of St. Lawrence, from the Strait of Belle Isle to Bonavista. The voyage was privately financed as the French monarchy had all its resources tied up in the Italian wars.

1508    Thomas Aubert of Dieppe explored the Gulf of St. Lawrence. He probably brought with him several Indians on his return to Rouen.

1509    It is recorded that a Norman navigator brought seven North American Indians to France. This may well have been Thomas Aubert of Dieppe.

1514    December 14. A declaration of the French monks regarding the collection of the tithe from the fishermen engaged along the Newfoundland cod banks read as follows: "... in as much in the Iceland, Newfoundland as elsewhere since sixty years." If this is interpreted one way it seems to indicate that Breton fishermen were off the coast of Newfoundland in 1454.

1515     Francis I became king of France. An ambitious monarch, he determined to challenge Spain and Portugal for domination of the New World. To a courtier the new king remarked: "God has not created those lands solely for Castilians."

1518     Baron de Léry made an abortive attempt to settle Sable Island off modern Canada. Cattle left behind when the colony foundered multiplied and later provided sustenance for other explorers and colonists.

1523     December. Giovanni de Verrazano, a Florentine in the service of the French monarch Francis I, sailed from Dieppe with a French crew under Captain Antoine de Conflans. Verrazano was to explore the New World and find a strait to Asia.

1524     March 5. Verrazano arrived off modern Wilmington, North Carolina. He sailed as far south as Charleston, South Carolina, and turned north to scrutinize the spacious harbors at New York and Newport, Rhode Island. The discoveries of Verrazano were used by Francis I to establish his legal claim to North America in his rivalry with Charles V of Spain.

1525     February 26. The French monarch, Francis I, was captured by Spanish troops at the Battle of Pavia. Imprisoned for thirteen months, Francis's absence from the throne meant that Verrazano's important voyage of discovery was not followed up by further French efforts in North America.

1527     August 3. John Rut counted eleven Norman, one Breton, and two Portuguese fishing vessels in the Bay of St. John, Newfoundland.

1529     The Peace of Cambrai gave France a breathing space after its long European wars. French resources were now available for exploration of the New World.

1534     April 20. Jacques Cartier sailed from St. Malo with two ships and sixty-two men. He was sent by Francis I to discover in North America mineral wealth comparable to that found by the Spanish in Mexico, and to find a sea passage to

Cathay. The voyage was financed by Phillippe de Brion-Chabot.

May 10. Jacques Cartier arrived off Newfoundland, meeting a vessel from Rochelle off the coast of Labrador.

July 24. Cartier's sailors erected a cross at the entrance to the Bay of Gaspé. Inscribing on it the words "VIVE LE ROY DE FRANCE," Cartier claimed "la nouvelle France" for his king. (See document, page 125).

August. Jacques Cartier returned home to St. Malo.

1535    May 19. Jacques Cartier, again financed by Phillippe de Brion-Chabot, sailed with 112 men in the Grande Hermine (126 tons), Petite Hermine (60 tons), and Emerillon (40 tons). Accompanied by Claude de Pontbriand, Charles de la Pommeraye, and other gentlemen, Cartier was commissioned by Francis I to search for Cathay via the St. Lawrence River.

August 10. Cartier was wind-blown in a small bay near the island of Anticosti on St. Lawrence's Day, thus the name he chose for the gulf and river of that name.

September 1. Cartier explored Labrador and moved up the St. Lawrence River. He reached the Saguenay River on September 1, and moved beyond to the Isle of Orléans. At Stadacona (modern Québec) he was received by Chief Donnacona with great ceremony.

October 2. Cartier reached Hochelaga (modern Montréal), where his 40 men were greeted by about 1,000 Indians. Songs, dances, and food were abundant, but despite the amiable reception Cartier was prevented by the lateness of the season from continuing his search for Cathay.

Winter. Cartier spent a horrible winter at Stadacona where about one-third of his men died. During the lean months from November, 1535, to April, 1536, many of the Indians became hostile and a severe scurvy epidemic swept the small band of explorers.

1536    May 3. Before leaving for France with the survivors of his expedition, Cartier erected a cross on the banks of the St. Lawrence to ensure the claims of the French monarchy.

Inscribed on the cross were the words "FRANCISCUS PRI-MUS, DEI GRATIA FRANCORUM REX REGNAT."

1540     By 1540 French fishermen completely dominated the fishing areas off Newfoundland.

January 15. Jean François de la Rocque, Sieur de Roberval, a nobleman from Picardy, was given 45,000 livres and a commission as the king's "lieutenant-general in the country of Canada."

February 6. The Sieur de Roberval took the oath of allegiance to the king and was charged with establishing a permanent colony in Canada.

October 17. Jacques Cartier was commissioned as captain-general and pilot of the fleet that Roberval was forming for the establishment of a colony in Canada. The king wanted the ships to sail by April 15, 1541.

1541     May 23. Jacques Cartier sailed for New France with three ships. Roberval, the appointed head of the French government in the New World, was to follow, but met with repeated delays. He did not leave France until April 16, 1542.

August 23. Cartier's three ships arrived at the Indian village of Stadacona. Two forts were erected and placed under the command of the Vicomte de Beaupré.

Winter. The French colony at Cap Rouge, near Québec, suffered severely with many colonists dying.

1542     April 16. The Sieur de Roberval left La Rochelle with three ships and 200 colonists to reinforce Cartier's small group at Québec.

June 8. Roberval entered the harbor of St. John. He counted seventeen fishing vessels, and sighted Cartier's ships returning to France. Cartier's voyage ended in total failure. He did not establish the permanent colony the king was expecting, and the iron pyrites ("fool's gold") and quartz crystals which he brought back in the belief that they were gold and diamonds discredited him in the eyes of the monarch.

1543     Roberval was recalled to France. The outbreak of religious wars in France meant that interest in the New World was neglected for a period. It was some sixty years before France attempted to found a permanent North American colony.

1544        With the failure to find gold and diamonds in Canada, most of the remaining colonists departed for France. A popular expression resulting from the failure of the Cartier-Roberval voyages was "false as a diamond from Canada."

1545        January-February. During the first two months of 1545 an average of two vessels per day left France for the Newfoundland fishing banks.

1547        Francis I died after having firmly established the right of France to explore, conquer, and settle unknown lands in North America. Though Spain and Portugal continued to cite the older papal bulls reserving rights in North America to them, it was an exercise in futility on their part.

1555        November. Admiral Gaspard de Coligny, a Protestant and first minister of Henri II, decided to establish a colony of Huguenots in the New World. The purpose was three-fold. In addition to establishing a sanctuary for fellow French Protestants, Coligny viewed his plan as establishing a base that could be expanded into a colonial empire, and weakening the powers of the Catholic nations by breaking the hold of Spain and Portugal on the New World. The expedition, which was aimed at the Rio de Janeiro area, was led by Nicolas Durand de Villegaignon. It failed.

1562        February 18. Jean Ribaut, a staunch Dieppe Protestant, sailed from Havre under orders from Admiral Coligny to establish a Huguenot colony in the New World and advance French claims to the "Terre des Bretons."

April 30. Jean Ribaut's colonists sighted the coast of Florida.

May 1. Ribaut landed near St. Augustine, Florida, and noted that the land appeared to be "the fairest, fruitfulest, and pleasantest of all the world." He left a column to mark his landfall.

Ribaut established an unsuccessful colony of thirty Huguenots at Port Royal, near Charleston, South Carolina. Ribaut sailed for France for supplies, but civil war prevented his return. Hunger and mutiny eventually broke up the colony two years later.

1564        With the conclusion of the civil wars in France, Admiral Coligny sent René de Laudonnière to establish a colony in Florida. With him came Jacques le Moyne, the first painter in the New World.

June 25. Laudonnière, with three vessels, arrived off the Carolina coast. He sailed south, finally establishing Fort Caroline near the mouth of the St. John River in Florida. Fort Caroline, built for protection against the Spanish, was a small, triangular structure of wood. Laudonnière graphically described the "cedars red as blood" and the "bay trees of so sovereign an odor that balm smells nothing like in comparison."

1565        Charles IX of France informed the Spanish ambassador that the coast of North America had been discovered by French subjects over one hundred years previously. It was called, he said, "Terre aux Bretons."

June 29. Pedro Menéndez de Avilés sailed from Cadiz with eleven ships under orders from Philip II of Spain to eradicate the colony of French Protestants in Florida.

August 28. Jean Ribaut arrived with seven ships, 300 men, and vital supplies that saved Fort Caroline, then on the verge of starvation and mutiny. On the same day Pedro Menéndez de Avilés landed near St. Augustine, which he founded September 8, with 2,600 Spanish soldiers and sailors.

September 4. The Spanish fleet under Menéndez de Avilés arrived at Fort Caroline. The French ships present weighed anchor and fled.

September 10. Ribaut sailed with all available able-bodied men to attack the Spanish camps, three miles away, from the sea.

September 11. Ribaut's fleet was becalmed off the entrance to the harbor where Menéndez's Spanish force was encamped. Menéndez decided to attack Fort Caroline overland with a force of 500 arquebusiers and pikemen.

September 19-20. In the evening the Spanish attacked Fort

Caroline killing about 142 men, women, and children, including prisoners. About 30 French escaped, including Laudonnière, to two ships anchored in the bay. The vessels, one commanded by Jacques Ribaut, the admiral's son, set sail for Europe where one landed at Rochelle and the other at Swansea, Wales. Fort Caroline was renamed San Mateo.

Jean Ribaut's fleet was wrecked between Matanzas and Cape Canaveral. The survivors formed into two groups to make their way to Fort Caroline because they were unaware of its capture by the Spanish.

October 9. Between 140 and 200 starving French survivors of Ribaut's shipwreck surrendered to Menéndez and 60 Spanish troops in hopes of mercy and a return to France because France and Spain were currently at peace. Twelve Bretons who professed to be Catholics and 4 carpenters and calkers needed by Menéndez were sent to the Spanish camp. The rest were slaughtered to the last man, their headless bodies being left for the carrion birds.

October 11. Menéndez, with 150 Spanish troops, met Ribaut with 350 French survivors. Some 200 French fled, but 150 surrendered to Menéndez in the belief he would aid them in leaving the area. Two gentlemen and 3 musicians were taken to the Spanish camp, but on the following day, October 12, the remainder of the French prisoners were hacked to death.

November 2. Menéndez, with 250 men, called on the French entrenched at Cape Canaveral to surrender. Several fled to friendly Indians, but the bulk accepted a pledge of safety. They were taken to St. Augustine and condemned to the galleys.

1567      August 22. Dominique de Gourgues set sail from the Clarente River with 100 arquebusiers and 80 sailors in three ships to avenge the massacre at Fort Caroline. Gourgues outfitted the expedition at his own expense by selling his possessions.

1568      April. A French force attacked a Spanish force of 400 on the River of May. The French captured one fort, killing all but a few prisoners, and the defenders of the second fort fled into the woods. The French followed, killing all but 15.

A French force captured San Mateo (formerly Fort Caroline)

from 250 Spanish defenders. Most of the Spaniards were slaughtered, with only a few fleeing to the hills. A few prisoners were hung on the site where Menéndez had hung captured Huguenots in 1565.

1578    By 1578 there were at least 150 French fishing vessels regularly off the Newfoundland coast. This did not include an additional 20 to 30 Biscayan whalers.

Henri III named a Breton nobleman, Mesqouez de la Roche, as governor, lieutenant-general, and viceroy of all lands in the New World. While there were not tangible results from this appointment, it marked a renewed interest in the New World by the French crown after a lapse of some thirty-four years.

1588    A twelve-year monopoly on the American fur trade was granted to Jacques Noel and Estienne Chaton. After a vociferous outcry from the St. Malo Bretons the grant was immediately cancelled.

1598    The Peace of Vervins brought all France under the influence of Henry of Navarre who sought to end the religious strife that was tearing France apart. As Henry IV he issued the Edict of Nantes which granted Huguenots equal civil status with Roman Catholics. By thus ending the divisive religious wars, Henry made it possible for France to again place emphasis on the New World.

Henry IV recommissioned the Marquis de la Roche to settle a colony in the New World. La Roche organized 200 men and 50 women, many from French prisons, to establish a colony on Sable Island, a small, sandy island ninety miles off Nova Scotia. Five years later, in 1603, 11 survivors were rescued and returned to France.

1599    Seeking to enlarge his kingdom with overseas colonies, Henry IV granted a trading monopoly in New France to Pierre Chauvin de Tonnetuit, a Norman merchant from Honfleur. The ten-year monopoly was granted on the condition that Chauvin establish a permanent colony and bring in fifty colonists per year. Although Chauvin died shortly afterward, the monopoly passed to Aymar de Chastes, governor of Dieppe.

1600    François Gravé, Sieur de Pont, (usually called Pontgravé) led an expedition that established a sixteen-man colony at Tadoussac, at the confluence of the Saguenay and St. Lawrence rivers. Pontgravé was under the patronage of Pierre Chauvin de Tonnetuit, and Pierre du Guast, Sieur de Monts. By the spring of 1601 only five members were still alive. This was the first attempt at a permanent French trading post in the New World. Previous attempts were of a temporary, seasonal nature. Nearly all of the early French efforts in the New World were commercial ventures.

As early as the first decade of the seventeenth century Samuel de Champlain, a former quartermaster in the army of Henry of Navarre, proposed that a canal link the Atlantic and Pacific Oceans via the Isthmus of Panama. He wrote: "In this spot of Panama, is gathered together, all the gold and silver which comes from Peru. It is freighted on a little river which flows from the mountains and which descends to Portovello, which is four leagues from Panama. One can judge that, if these four leagues of land were cut, one could come from the south sea to the sea this side."

1603     The Duc de Montmorency commissioned the Sieur de Monts as vice-admiral of lands in Acadia and along both sides of the St. Lawrence River from Gaspé as far inland as could be explored.

March 15. Pontgravé and Samuel de Champlain set sail for Tadoussac with two ships. It was to be the first of eleven such voyages for the durable and energetic Champlain.

June 11. Samuel de Champlain began exploring the Saguenay River, advancing thirty to forty miles upstream from Tadoussac.

June 23. Pontgravé and Champlain observed and named the falls of Montmorency. They continued exploring as far up the St. Lawrence as the Lachine Rapids at Montreal.

September. The Sieur de Roberval reached Sable Island to rescue the eleven surviving members of his colony, established in 1598.

November 8. Henry IV commissioned Pierre du Guast, Sieur de Monts, as lieutenant-general of Canada. He received a ten-year trade monopoly in what is today Nova Scotia and New Brunswick, for the purpose of settling those areas.

1604    Pierre du Guast, Sieur de Monts, a Huguenot, was named
        viceroy and captain-general in New France. He received
        a fur-trading monopoly in Acadia on the condition that he
        establish 100 settlers per year in that area. The area of
        the monopoly included the land from Cape Breton south be-
        yond New York.

        February 10. The Sieur de Monts organized a commercial
        company among the citizens of Rouen, Rochelle, and Saint
        Jean de Luz.

        April 7. De Monts, with Sieur de Poutrincourt and Samuel
        de Champlain, set sail from Havre de Grace for Acadia.
        Pontgravé was to follow with supplies in a few days.

        June 25. De Monts raised the first French colors hoisted in
        Acadia. This settlement was located at Passamaquoddy Bay,
        on the island of St. Croix, at the mouth of the St. Croix
        River. Half of the settlers died during the first winter.

1605    The winter of 1605-06 was relatively mild compared with
        previous winters. Champlain marveled that "only a quarter
        of the people died."

1606    The patent of the Sieur de Monts was revoked because of
        complaints from Basques and Bretons.

        November 14. Le Théâtre de Neptune en la Nouvelle-France
        was the first theatrical production in America. It was per-
        formed by the small group of colonists near Port Royal,
        Acadia.

1607    Merchants from port cities in northern France, after suc-
        ceeding in obtaining the revocation of a monopoly granted to
        De Monts, began opening the fur trade in New France.

1608    April 5. Pontgravé sailed from Honfleur, his ships loaded
        with goods for the trading post at Tadoussac. Upon his ar-
        rival he was attacked by Basque fur traders who killed one
        man and wounded Pontgravé and two of his men.

        April 13. Samuel de Champlain sailed for Tadoussac in the
        barque Don de Dieu.

        June 3. Champlain arrived at Tadoussac in time to negoti--
        ate a peace settlement with Basque fur traders who earlier
        attacked Pontgravé's fleet.

July 3. Samuel de Champlain founded a colony at Québec. He was the first French leader in the New World to make genuine colonization his primary motivation, rather than fishing or fur trading.

September 18. Pontgravé left for France, leaving Champlain's colony to winter in Québec. Disease and hostility of Basque traders at Tadoussac killed all but eight of Champlain's company.

1609      June 8. Pontgravé arrived back in Tadoussac with supplies from France. Only eight of Champlain's twenty-eight settlers were still alive.

June 18. Champlain ascended the St. Lawrence River with a party of French and Indians. They met between 200 and 300 Hurons and Algonquins on a war raid against the Iroquois and joined them in a march down the Richelieu River.

June 28. Champlain, with eleven French and a large number of Indians, headed down the Richelieu River. All of the French, including Morais and La Routte, were armed with arquebuses.

July 30. Near Ticonderoga, Champlain with 2 French and about 60 Indian allies met some 200 Iroquois. Champlain fired his arquebus, loaded with four balls, killing 2 Indians and wounding another. A second shot sent the incredulous Iroquois fleeing, and gained for the French their undying hatred. It was on this same trip that Champlain discovered the lake that today bears his name.

1610      Henry IV was assassinated.

Jean de Biencourt de Poutrincourt landed a shipload of colonists at Port Royal. Included in this group was a secular priest, Jessé Flesché, who baptized some eighty Micmac Indians within a few weeks of his arrival. This began the great missionary drive by French clergy in the New World.

August 8. Champlain, after receiving news of the death of Henry IV, left Québec for Honfleur. Sixteen men remained at Québec under du Parc.

September 27. Champlain arrived in Honfleur to look after his New World interests on the death of Henry IV.

1611            January 26. The first Jesuits set sail from France for the
                French colony in North America.

                May 13. Champlain arrived back at Tadoussac. Within a
                few days thirteen ships arrived to reinforce him, with more
                on the way. Champlain later explored the St. Lawrence in
                an effort to arrange for a permanent fur trade. He founded
                a trading post near modern Montréal.

1612            October 8. The Comte de Soissons was appointed viceroy
                of Canada. He died after commissioning Champlain as his
                deputy, and was replaced by the Prince de Condé.

                November 13. The letters-patent to the Prince de Condé
                were signed at Paris.

                November 22. Champlain was commissioned as the deputy
                of the Prince de Condé in North America.

1613            March 12. The ship Jonas sailed from Honfleur with forty-
                eight sailors and colonists, including two Jesuits, Father
                Quentin and Brother Gilbert du Thet. The ship was sent by
                Madame de Guercheville to establish a Jesuit mission on
                the Penobscot River near present day Bangor, Maine. Cap-
                tain Charles Fleury commanded the Jonas, and a courtier
                named La Saussaye headed the colonists. Because the crew
                refused to go on land, the mission of St. Sauveur was es-
                tablished on the mainland, across from Mont Désert Island,
                where it was vulnerable from the sea.

                May 8. Champlain and Nicholas de Vignau arrived at Québec
                from France. They proceeded to explore the Ottawa River,
                promising aid to the Hurons and Algonquins against the Iro-
                quois. From the beginning of French influence in North
                America it was their policy to participate in Indian politics,
                hold the balance of power between the tribes, and include
                all of the remotest tribes under their influence and economic
                control.

                July 2. Samuel Argall of Virginia, with the fourteen-gun
                ship Treasurer, and sixty soldiers, destroyed the St. Sau-
                veur mission without warning.

                July 8. Champlain sailed from Tadoussac, arriving at St.
                Malo on August 26.

October. Samuel Argall of Virginia razed Acadia.

1614       The French Estates-General approved sending four Récollets, a branch of the Franciscans, to Canada. Some 1,500 livres were provided to defray expenses.

Jean Vigné, of Huguenot descent, became the first European child born on Manhattan Island.

1615       It is estimated that by 1615 over 500 French vessels sailed annually to the whale and cod fishing and fur trading areas of New France.

April 24. Champlain sailed from Honfleur for Québec with four members of the Récollet order.

May. Champlain arrived at Québec. He brought with him the Récollet priests Dennis Jamay, Jean d'Olbeau and Joseph le Caron, and the lay brother Pacifique du Plessis. The Récollets, a mendicant order, were a reform branch of the Franciscans.

June 15. The Récollet Father Jean d'Olbeau officiated at the first Mass celebrated in a small chapel built at Québec. The four Récollets soon split, Le Caron joining the Hurons, d'Olbeau going to the Montagnais, while Jamay and du Plessis remained to succor the French and Indians about Québec. They met, at best, with indifference from their prospective Indian converts. They were no doubt more important for their early explorations, Le Caron preceding Champlain to Georgian Bay, where he constructed a chapel.

Champlain, accompanying a great war party of Northern Indians, first viewed Lake Huron.

October 10. Champlain, with a large war party of Hurons, attacked a fortified Onondaga village on Lake Oneida, near present Syracuse. The Hurons lacked coordination in their attacks, and the French proved largely ineffective. Champlain suffered a severe defeat, being himself wounded in the knee and ankle. Some historians believe that the Iroquois defenders were Oneidas, and others advance the claim that the attack took place against the Seneca in Madison County. In any case, it caused many Hurons to doubt the wisdom of their French alliance.

1616        Champlain left Tadoussac to report in France, arriving at
            Honfleur on September 10.

1617        Champlain appealed to the French Chamber of Commerce
            for a major colonizing effort in the New World. He but-
            tressed his requests by citing the economic benefits to be
            gained from such products as fish, fur, timber, minerals,
            grain, and leather, which he valued at some 6,400,000 livres
            per year. He sought 400 families and a garrison of 300 sol-
            diers for Québec. His hopes could not be realized because
            Louis XIII was faced with rebellion of the great lords, the
            rising power of the Huguenots, and the beginning of the
            Thirty Years' War across the Rhine River.

            Louis Hébert, a Parisian druggist, arrived in Québec with
            his wife and three children. He became the first real "habi-
            tant" farmer at Québec.

1620        Among the Pilgrims on the Mayflower was Priscilla Mullins,
            daughter of William Mullins, who was orginally a Huguenot
            named Guillaume Molines. Her later marriage to John Al-
            den produced the famous New England Allen family. Included
            in this line of descent was John Adams, a president of the
            United States. There is, in addition, reason to believe that
            Alden himself was of Huguenot stock.

            June 3. The Récollets laid the cornerstone of a building on
            the St. Charles River opposite Québec, six months before
            the Pilgrims began their celebrated meetinghouse at Ply-
            mouth. The oldest French church in North America, it was
            built in the style of the Norman frame dwellings destined
            to be the standard housing in French North America.

1621        Phillip de la Noye arrived in Plymouth, Massachusetts,
            aboard the ship Fortune. His descendants became important
            in the United States under the Anglicized version of his
            name, Delano.

1622        Father Joseph le Caron, with another Récollet, Father Nico-
            las Viel, and a lay brother, Gabriel Sagard, journeyed west
            from Québec through the Huron country. Sagard became the
            historian of the Récollet mission.

1623        The Niew Nederlandt sailed for the New World with thirty
            families, including Walloons and Huguenots, who landed and
            spread throughout Connecticut, Delaware, and New York.

1624        At Trois Rivières Champlain negotiated a peace treaty be-
            tween the Hurons, Algonquins, Montagnais, and Iroquois.

1625        Cardinal Richelieu decided to reinforce the missions in Can-
            ada with missionaries from the militant Society of Jesus.
            He remained devoted to the development of New France
            throughout the remainder of his life.

            Henri de Lévy, Duc de Ventadour, purchased the title of
            viceroy of New France and banned all but those of the Ro-
            man Catholic religion.

            Five Jesuits were dispatched to Québec, with three more
            following in 1626. They were greatly hampered by Huguenot
            merchants who controlled the shipping at La Rochelle and
            refused to aid the Catholic missionaries after the Duc de
            Ventadour excluded Protestants from Canada.

            The first black-robed French Jesuits arrived in Québec led
            by Father Le Jeune. They included Charles Lalemant, Jean
            de Brébeuf, Enemond Massé, François Charton, Gilbert Bu-
            rel, and one who was unknown. Denied the aid of the Crown,
            the Récollets determined to cooperate with these new mis-
            sionaries of the Society of Jesus.

            September 1. The Jesuits occupied the ground at the conflu-
            ence of the Lairet and St. Charles rivers. Their new home
            was completed April 6, 1626.

1626        Father La Roche Daillon, with two interpreters, including
            one named Grenoble, explored the country of the Neutrals.

            It is estimated that between 15,000 and 22,000 furs passed
            through Québec. They sold for an average of 10 livres
            apiece in France. Calculating the costs of maintaining 40
            traders at Québec, two supply ships, 150 sailors, supplies
            and trade goods, the cost of the year's operations was about
            100,000 livres. This yielded a minimum profit of 50,000 to
            120,000 livres.

            April 6. The Jesuits completed their new home on the St.
            Charles River.

            May 4. Peter Minuit arrived in New Amsterdam. A Huguenot,
            he purchased Manhattan Island from the Indians and became
            the first "Dutch" governor of the New Netherland.

August 1. Father Lalemant, in a letter to France, said that
there were only forty-three French in Québec.

1627

April 29. In an attempt to revitalize New France, Cardinal
Richelieu revoked all previous trading concessions and privileges. The economic future of the colony was placed in
the hands of the Company of New France, better known as
the Company of One Hundred Associates. The company was
required to provide for an annual emigration of 300 colonists
to New France, and was required to furnish agricultural
equipment for their livelihood.

1628

April. Four armed vessels and a fleet of eighteen transports
sailed from Dieppe under the command of Claude de Roquemont. They carried colonists, supplies, and thirty-five cannons for the defenses at Québec. The expedition was the
first under the sponsorship of the Hundred Associates.

May 6. The French Council of State ratified the charter of
the Hundred Associates. Thereafter, no Calvinist was permitted to emigrate to New France.

A number of London merchants funded a private expedition
to seize Québec from France. Led by Gervase Kirke, the
small fleet's three vessels were commanded by his sons,
David, Lewis, and Thomas.

The first French religious service was held in New York.

1629

Jean Nicolet, a native of Cherbourg, left Québec to live among
the Nipissings in order to learn their language and customs.
He spent eight or nine years traveling among the Indians,
settling down at Trois Rivières only in 1637.

April 23. A peace treaty was signed between France and
England, one article of which stated that all conquests after
April 24, 1629, would be negated and returned to their for-
mer owners.

July. Admiral Kirke arrived off New France, capturing nineteen French fishing vessels, eighteen transports under
Claude de Roquemont, and numerous other prizes.

Destitute for supplies, Champlain surrendered Québec to the
English admiral, Gervase Kirke. During the English occupation of Québec, 1629-32, the Jesuits and Récollets were

forced to leave New France. When Québec reverted to
French control, due to the peace signed April 23, 1629, only
the Jesuits returned. Thus ended the Récollet presence in
New France.

1632    Récollet lay brother Gabriel Sagard published his first book
about North America, Le Grand Voyage du Pays des Hurons
(Paris). It was, in effect, a history of the Récollet missions.

March 29. Louis XIII and Charles I signed the Treaty of St.
Germain-en-Laye, one provision of which stated that England surrender all territories taken from France in North
America. This included Québec, which Champlain had surrendered to the Kirkes in 1629. It also included the French
settlement at Port Royal.

April 18. Two Jesuits, Paul le Jeune and Anne de la Nouë,
sailed from Havre with a fleet under Émery de Caen for
Québec. Louis XIII confirmed the right of the Jesuits to
conduct missionary work in New France. In addition, the
monarch forbade foreigners and Huguenots from migrating
to New France.

July 5. Émery de Caen anchored before Québec to reclaim
it for the French crown. He was compensated for his losses
during the war with England by a one-year monopoly on the
fur trade. At the end of that period the fur trade would be
placed under the control of the Hundred Associates.

August 28. Jesuit Paul le Jeune penned a letter detailing to
his superiors his experiences in North America. This was
the first of the Jesuit Relations, from which we have gained
most of the knowledge that we have of New France during
the following forty years. Dispatched singly or in pairs to
the Hurons, Algonquins, Abenakis, Iroquois, Chippewas, Ot-
tawas, Illinois, and scores of other Indian tribes, the Jesuit
missionaries were required to submit annual reports to
their superior between 1632 and 1673. This narrative, published in Paris, besides providing valuable historical information, evoked great contemporary interest in the missions
of New France.

May 23. Champlain arrived at Québec with a commission
as governor from Cardinal Richelieu. Ruling on behalf of
the Hundred Associates, Champlain brought with him Father
Jean de Brébeuf and the first company of royal troops ever
sent to New France.

June 23. Father Jean Nicolet returned to Québec from the country of the Nipissings to report on Indian affairs in the west.

1634 Jesuits Jean Nicolet and Jean de Brébeuf journeyed west to the Huron nation and beyond. Nicolet visited the Nipissings and Chippewas, stopped at Michilimackinac, explored Lake Michigan and ascended the Fox River. Landing in what he thought at first must be China, he learned that it was the area around Green Bay, Wisconsin. His "Chinese" were friendly Winnebagoes. Brébeuf organized at Ihontahira, near Thunder Bay, the greatest of all Indian missions in New France.

Trois Rivières was built as a fur trading center.

June. Father Buteux and two other priests arrived at Québec. At a time when there were already 4,000 permanent British settlers in Massachusetts alone, there numbered only 60 French people in all of Canada. The English were already attached to the soil. The French came only seasonally in the summer.

1635 Robert Giffard became the first French Seigneur in North America when he established his censitaires along the Côte de Beaupré, on the north shore of the St. Lawrence below Québec. Under the seigniorial system, which became popular in New France, the seigneurs held lands in trust from the king. They, in turn, distributed lands in trust to censitaires who settled it. The purpose was to stimulate colonization, which the formation of companies had failed to do.

December 25. Samuel de Champlain died in Québec at the age of sixty-eight. The eulogy was read by Father Le Jeune, and a tomb was erected to his honor.

1636 Gabriel Sagard published, in Paris, an enlarged version of his work on the Récollet missions in North America, Histoire du Canada.

March. Charles Hualt, Sieur de Montmagny, succeeded Champlain as governor of New France. He arrived in June and concentrated on consolidating the existing colony, rather than fostering new explorations as Champlain had done.

1637 Johannes La Montagne, a Huguenot, probably became the first physician in New Amsterdam.

Jean Nicolet returned from his mission among the western Indians and settled at Trois Rivières. He died in 1642.

August. Drought and pestilence among the Hurons were attributed by the Indians to the presence in their midst of the mysterious Jesuits. A great Huron council was held in August, 1637, with Father Brébeuf narrowly escaping martyrdom.

1639   La Mére Marie, a member of the Norman haute noblesse and of great wealth, gave up her position and fortune in France to establish the Ursuline Convent at Québec. She was benefactor and leader of a teaching order, under the name La Mére Marie de l'Incarnation. It was soon followed by the Hospitalières, a nursing order.

October. By October, 1639, twenty-seven French missionaries and assistants were living among the Hurons, including thirteen Jesuits.

1640   The population of Québec included sixty-four families, or a total of 356 people. Included in this number were 29 Jesuits, 53 soldiers, 116 women, and 158 men.

The chapel of Nôtre Dame de Recouvrance, built by Champlain to commemorate the recovery of Québec from the English, burned. The early records of Québec, stored there, were lost.

1641   Father Isaac Jogues and Charles Raymbault accompanied a party of Chippewa to the junction of Lakes Huron and Superior and became the first missionaries to preach on the shores of Lake Superior. They named the Sault de Sainte Marie in honor of the Virgin Mary. Raymbault died in September.

1642   The European population of Canada numbered about 300.

Paul de Chomedy, Sieur de Maisonneuve, with forty-two followers, dedicated a mission named Ville Marie. It grew to become the modern city of Montréal. Jeanne Mance, who accompanied Maisonneuve, ran a hospital in Montréal, and Marguerite Bourgeoys began there, in a vacant stable, the first school of the Sisters of Our Lady.

September 29. René Goupil, a lay companion of Father Jogues,

was tomahawked to death by the Mohawk Indians at Ossernenon, modern Auriesville, New York. After being tortured
and treated as a slave, Jogues eventually escaped to the
Dutch post at Fort Orange (Albany).

1645      The merchants in New France formed the Company of the
Colony, which obtained a virtual monopoly on the fur trade
by paying the Company of New France twenty-five percent
of its gross receipts. While it attempted to systematize
the fur trade, it also eliminated many small traders and
hurt the traffic conducted by the habitants. It operated until the destruction of the Huron settlements in 1650.

1646      Father Isaac Jogues and John Lalande, a lay missionary,
were martyred by the Mohawk Indians at Ossernenon, modern Auriesville, New York.

Iroquois war parties began a series of violent assaults that
virtually destroyed the Huron nation by 1649.

1647      The Basilica in Québec was built as the headquarters for
the French church in North America. Burned in 1922, it was
rebuilt in 1925.

1648      Mohawk and Seneca war parties destroyed the primary Huron villages, crippling the French allies in Canada.

Father Daniel was martyred by the Iroquois.

1649      March 16. A war party of 1,000 Mohawks and Senecas razed
the Huron villages of St. Louis and St. Ignace, capturing
Fathers Jean de Brébeuf and Gabriel Lalemant. After being
tortured with boiling water, red-hot hatchets, and fire,
both were killed.

1650      Father Druillettes, S.J., conferred with Governor Bradford
of Massachusetts regarding the possibility of a peace treaty
between New France and New England. New England wanted
a commercial treaty, but not a treaty aimed against the Iroquois. No agreement was signed.

1651      Spring. The defeat of the Neutral nation, friendly toward
France, was completed when a large village of 1,600 Neu-
trals was captured by the Iroquois and all adult males put
to the hatchet.

1652   An Iroquois assault by 600 warriors on Trois Rivières was
beaten off by a garrison of 40, many not yet out of their
teens. The governor of the small fort was killed along with
21 of the settlers and soldiers.

Isaac Bethlo arrived in New Amsterdam from Calais. His
name, Anglicized to Bedloe, was given to Bedloe's Island in
New York Harbor. This was the same island where, over
200 years later, the Statue of Liberty, a gift of the French
people, was erected.

1653   The European population of Canada numbered about 2,000.

The western tribes defeated a large Iroquois invasion force,
causing the Iroquois to sue for peace with New France. This
was important because it reopened French trade routes between Montréal and the West.

1654   The first Indian trading fleet in several years reached Montréal.

July. Father Simon le Moyne journeyed down the Oswego
River into the heart of the Iroquois nations.

1655   The Iroquois began the destruction of the Erie Nation, which
they completed in 1656.

During a period of peace, a Boston expedition of four ships
and 500 men attacked Acadia, capturing Port Royal and
French trading posts along the St. John and Penobscot rivers.

November 3. By the Treaty of Westminister, France and
England agreed to negotiate the Acadian matter, and if necessary, to submit it to the arbitration of the Republic of
Hamburg. England finally relinquished its claim to Acadia
in 1670.

1656   By 1656 the French population in New Amsterdam was so
large it was necessary to issue all government proclama-
tions in Dutch and French.

July 17. French Jesuits built the first building on the site
of modern Syracuse, New York.

Pierre d'Esprit, Sieur de Radisson, and Médard Chouart,
Sieur de Grosseilliers, explored west from Montréal. They

probably visited Green Bay and explored deep into the Illinois country.

1657 Large groups of French Protestants arrived in New Netherland during the period 1657-63.

July 26. Following a peace treaty with the Iroquois, a colony of French left Montreal to spend the winter in the Onondaga country. The explorers included Médard Chouart, Sieur de Grosseilliers, and Pierre d'Esprit, Sieur de Radisson.

1658 New Haarlem was founded. It included many Walloons and Huguenots.

The Vicomte d'Argenson arrived in Canada as the new governor.

Pierre d'Esprit, Sieur de Radisson, and Médard Chouart, Sieur de Grosseilliers, travelled west, exploring the area until 1660. Moving via the Sault Ste. Marie and Lake Michigan, they explored Chequamegon Bay, Wisconsin, and established the first known European habitation in Wisconsin. They apparently visited Sioux villages in eastern Minnesota, whom they enticed into trading with New France. Early in 1660 they led a force of 100 trading canoes east from the Sault Ste. Marie to Montréal.

1659 A Huguenot church was founded in New York.

Radisson and Grosseilliers became the first Europeans to view the Mississippi Basin. They explored Lake Superior, visiting the lands of the Sioux, Assiniboines, and Creeks. They helped to fix the firm hold of the Hudson's Bay Company on the northern fur trade.

June. François Xavier de Laval de Montigny arrived at Québec as bishop and vicar-apostolic. As the chief religious authority in New France, Laval favored the Jesuits and fought against the traffic in liquor.

1660 An early census of Canada showed 3,418 Europeans in New France at a time when New England numbered just under 80,000 people.

Father René Ménard, with his donné, Jean Guerin, penetrated Lake Superior accompanied by the fur trader Antoine Trot-

tier and several companions. The traders included Jean
François Pouteret (Sieur de Bellecourt), Adrien Jolliet,
Claude David, Pierre Levasseur (l'Espèrance), and Laflêche.
The name of a seventh was not preserved.

A force of sixty large trading canoes reached Montréal
from the Sault Ste. Marie. Radisson estimated the value of
the furs at $60,000, but others felt the value might be as high
as $400,000. In those days even the lesser of these figures
was a huge fortune.

Some 800 Iroquois attacked Montréal, but Dollard, the commander at Ft. Ville Marie, met them thirty miles up the
Ottawa River at a local Indian palisade. With 16 French and
44 Indians under the Huron and Algonquin Chiefs Anohotaha
and Mitiwemeg, he held out for ten days, saving Montréal
in what has been called the Canadian "Thermopylae."

October. Radisson and Grosseilliers followed a northern
tributary of Lake Superior to Lake Nepigon.

1661          Half of the residents of Haarlem, in New Netherland, were
              Huguenots.

              Louis XIII assumed the reins of government in person when
              Cardinal Mazarin died. The administration of the colonies
              was entrusted to Jean Baptiste Colbert, a man of vision and
              experience in developing commercial and agricultural af-
              fairs. Pierre Boucher, chosen by the colonists to represent
              them, detailed the agricultural and mineral wealth of New
              France. His report created a new interest in New France
              as a rich, permanent possession, rather than simply a trad-
              ing post.

              Baron Dubois d'Avaugour was named governor of Québec,
              but a controversy with Laval over the sale of liquor to the
              Indians brought about his recall. He was replaced by the
              Sieur de Mézy in 1663.

1662          John Touton received permission to establish a Huguenot
              colony in Massachusetts. It was customary for people not
              of English origin to appeal to the English government for
              permission to create settlements in the English colonies.
              (See document, page 127).

              Louis XIV's Finance Minister, Colbert, urged the monarch

to expand French colonization in Canada. Louis reorganized New France under the leadership of a governor, appointive council, and intendant, the latter being the king's personal representative.

Robert Cavelier, Sieur de la Salle, established Fort Prud-'homme near where modern Memphis, Tennessee, stands.

1663  New France became a royal province, with a total European population of less than 3,000 people

Finance Minister Colbert sent a party of agricultural colonists with John Boucher to New France. Believing that the old charter of the Company of New France was detrimental to the development of the colony, he revoked it and persuaded the monarch to send a royal agent to report on affairs in the North American colony. In addition, he sent a regiment of regular troops for the defense of New France. The royal commissioner was the Sieur Gaudais-Dupont; the new governor was the Chevalier de Mézy.

Jean Baptiste Talon, intendant of New France, used his position to dominate the government from 1663-1672. Under his leadership, nearly 30,000 French migrated to Québec.

François de Laval, the bishop of New France, founded the university that still bears his name.

A tremendously destructive earthquake occurred in Canada, causing many colonists to raise the cry "Back to France."

Thirty-five canoes, with 150 Indians and 7 French traders, left the Sault Ste. Marie with furs for Montréal. They brought with them a large ingot of copper made by the Indians, the first indication of copper on Lake Superior.

March 26. Monseigneur François de Montmorency-Laval, the first bishop of New France, decreed the erection of the Seminary of Quebec.

September 18. The governor, Sieur de Mézy, issued an edict prohibiting the sale of liquor to the Indians. It was a triumph for Bishop Laval and the Jesuits.

1664  French Finance Minister Colbert created La Compagnie des Indes Occidentales, which included all French possessions in America. Alexander de Prouville, Marquis de Tracy, was appointed to be lieutenant-general of all lands in North America. For New France, Daniel de Rémy, Sieur de Courcelles, was appointed governor and Jean Baptiste Talon, intendant.

New Netherland, which supplied armaments and ammunition to the Iroquois, was ceded to Charles II of England. Charles II was the ally and pensioner of Louis XIV, thus tensions between the Iroquois and the French were relieved.

1665          The population of New France reached 3,215.

Jean Baptiste Talon, intendant of New France, asked the king for prospective brides for the five-to-one male population in New France. The first consignment of "Filles du Roy" was chosen from the Royal Orphanage in Paris. Later, several shiploads of Norman peasants arrived in New France. Land was also offered to all who would settle near the Richelieu River.

Ft. Chambly was constructed for the protection of the Richelieu River.

June 30. The Marquis de Tracy arrived at Québec as lieutenant-general for North America. Arriving at nearly the same time were companies of the Règiment de Carignan-Salières, veterans of the Turkish wars, and the first regiment of regular troops for the defense of Québec. By the end of the year, 1,300 officers and men had taken up residence in New France.

August 8. Claude Jean Allouez, S.J., explored beyond the Great Lakes and heard for the first time of a great river called the "Missipi." Appointed vicar-general in the west by Bishop Laval, he spent the next twenty-four years traveling about Wisconsin and Illinois. He wrote a prayer book in the Illinois language for Father Marquette. Allouez became known as "the Apostle of the Ottawa Missions."

1666          The census in New France indicated 3,418 European settlers.

Fort La Motte was constructed on the Richelieu River.

January. French forces marched south to force a peace on the Mohawks. The French unexpectedly ran into a British outpost near Schenectady, but both sides parted after peaceful compliments. The Senecas, Oneidas, and Onondagas sent emissaries to Québec to sue for peace.

1667   France regained permanent title to Acadia by the Treaty of Breda.

Summer. The Iroquois, defeated twice by the western Indians and no longer receiving arms from the Dutch, came to Québec to sue for peace.

1668   The population of New France reached 5,870.

Nicolas Perrot explored among the Algonquins around Green Bay. He formed a series of alliances with the tribes in central Wisconsin and the upper Mississippi, which laid the foundation for French sovereignty in the Northwest. Perrot broke the Ottawa monopoly on western furs, discovered lead mines along the Mississippi, and claimed all of the Sioux lands for the French monarchy.

Jacques Marquette, excited by reading the Jesuit Relations, received an appointment to New France. He and Father Dablon founded a mission on the south side of the Sault Ste. Marie, the earliest mission in what is today Michigan.

1669   July 6. René Robert Cavelier, Sieur de la Salle, left Montréal with twenty men in seven canoes and headed up the St. Lawrence with the intention of exploring the vast river to the west, the Mississippi. In 1669-70 he pushed French power into the Ohio Valley.

1670   Richard Batin, Jacques Jours and Richard Deyos settled in Charleston, South Carolina, in the year in which it was founded.

La Salle reached the Ohio River, which he called "La Belle Rivière." He descended it as far as modern Louisville.

Phillip l'Anglois settled in Salem, Massachusetts. As Philip English he became one of Salem's most influential merchants and was instrumental in bringing other Huguenots to Salem, including John Touzel, John Browne (Jean le Brun), Nicholas Chevalier, Peter Morall, Edward Feveryear, John Voudin, Rachel Dellaclose, and the Valpy, Lefavor, and Cabot families.

1672            Canada had a population of 7,200.

                Father Albanel became the first European to reach Hudson's
                Bay by the overland route from the St. Lawrence.

                April. Louis de Baude, Comte de Frontenac, was appointed
                governor of New France. He brought a new, strong spirit to
                North America, serving two terms from 1672-82 and 1689-
                98.

                December. Sieur Louis Joliet brought Father Marquette in-
                structions to explore the Mississippi.

1673            Fort Frontenac was constructed on Lake Ontario.

                May 17. Louis Joliet, a trader and prospector, and Jacques
                Marquette, S.J., left Mackinac to explore the Mississippi.

                June 14. Joliet and Marquette entered the Wisconsin River.

                June 17. Joliet and Marquette reached the Mississippi, which
                the former named "La Baude" for the family of the Comte
                de Frontenac. Marquette, the Jesuit, called it "Conception,"
                and recorded the native name as "Missipi."

                July 17. Joliet and Marquette turned back toward the north
                because they feared running into hostile Spaniards below the
                Arkansas River. Marquette estimated their southernmost
                position at 33° 41'.

1674            From 1674 to 1691 the French had a virtual monopoly on
                North American tobacco.

                December 4. Father Jacques Marquette constructed the first
                dwelling on the site of modern Chicago, Illinois.

1675            May 18. Jacques Marquette, S.J., died on the eastern shore
                of Lake Michigan.

1677            Catherine Tekakwirha, the "Lily of the Mohawk," took up
                residence near Montréal to study Catholicism.

                A group of Huguenot settlers purchased a tract of land from
                Indian owners and founded New Paltz, New York. The price
                of the transaction included "40 kettles (10 large & 30 small),
                forty axes, forty adzes; forty shirts; four hundred fathoms

of white network; sixty pairs of stockings (half small sizes);
one hundred bars of lead; one keg of powder; one hundred
knives; four kegs of wine; forty oars; forty pieces of 'duffel'
(heavy woolen cloth); sixty blankets; one hundred needles;
one hundred awls; one measure of tobacco; two horses--
one stallion, one mare."

1678        September 1. Daniel Greysolon, Sieur du Luth, left Montréal
on a three year expedition to the Sioux country. He returned
to Québec in 1681.

December. The Griffon, the first ship to operate on Lake
Ontario, carried the Sieur de la Salle from Fort Frontenac
to the straits of Niagara where he constructed a crude fort.
This was later the site of the stone fortress commanding
the western route along the Lake Ontario-Lake Erie trading
passage.

1679        Charles II urged the Huguenots in England to migrate to
South Carolina "to raise grapes, olives and silkworms."

The Sieur de la Salle sailed the first ship, Le Griffon, from
Lake Erie to Green Bay. Loaded with furs, it foundered on
the return voyage.

The Sieur de la Salle, along with Henri de Tonti, explored
the Illinois River to Peoria, establishing Fort Crèvecoeur
at Starved Rock. Disease and desertion thinned the French
ranks and Tonti finally abandoned the fort in the face of a
mutiny.

The Sieur de la Salle named Louisiana in honor of Louis
XIV of France.

July 2. In the Isanti village on Lake Millelac, the Sieur du
Luth erected the royal arms and took possession of the Sioux
country for Louis XIV.

September 15. Daniel Greysolon, Sieur du Luth, arranged a
peace between the Sioux, Chippewa and the other tribes around
Lake Superior. This was of great importance to French exploration and the fur trade. Among his party were the Sieur
le Maistre, Paul la Vigne, Sieur Bellegarde, Sieur de la Rue,
Faffart, and the brothers Pepin. The Great Council was held
between the Sioux and Assiniboins, at war for thirty years,
at the head of Lake Superior.

1680    Large scale Huguenot immigration took place in Charleston,
South Carolina, beginning with the arrival of forty-five people. This movement, lasting from 1680 to 1686, included
the following families: Bayard, Bonneau, Benoit, Bocquet, Ba-
cot, Chevalier, Corde, Chastaquier, Duprè, Deslisles, Dubose,
Dutarque, de la Coursillière, Dubouxdieu, Fayssaux, Gaillard,
Gendron, Horry, Guignard, Huger, Legaré, Lauren, Lausac,
Marion, Mazycq, Manigault, Mallichamp, Neuville, Péronneau,
Porcher, Peyre, Ravenel, Saint Julien, and Trevezant. They
were sent by the Proprietors to produce wine and silk, the
first forty-five being brought in the English frigate <u>Rich-
mond</u>.

Jacques Tiphaine, ancestor of the Tiffany family, came to
New York about 1680.

1681    Father Louis Hennepin explored the upper Mississippi.

1682    Rev. Peter Daillé, later called the "Apostle of the Huguenots
in America, " was sent by the Bishop of London to minister
to French Protestants in the New World.

The Comte de Frontenac was recalled due to quarrels with
the bishop and intendant in New France.

April 9. The Sieur de la Salle reached the mouth of the Mis-
sissippi River where he took possession of Louisiana for
France, erected a column with a fleur-de-lis, and buried
a lead tablet inscribed thusly: "LUDOVICUS MAGNUS REG-
NAT NONO APRILIS 1682. " The reverse read: "ROBERTUS
CAVELIER, CUM DOMINO DE TONTI, LEGATO, R. R.
ZENOBIO MEMBRE, RECOLLECTO, ET VIGINTI GALLIS,
PRIMUS HOC FLUMEN, INDE AB ILINEORUM PARO EN-
AVIGAVIT, EJUSQUE OSTIUM FECIT PERVIUM NONO
APRILIS 1682."

December. Fort St. Louis, Illinois, was established by La
Salle and Tonti.

1683    Between 1683 and 1702 New Paltz, New York, was so heavily
French that the church records were kept in the French language.

Governor de la Barre invited the Iroquois chiefs to a confer-
ence in Montréal, but there were no positive results. The
Iroquois wanted removal of the French forts along the Great
Lakes and were not impressed by a French show of force.

1684    The Jesuit mission at Kaskaskia was established.

July. Governor de la Barre led an expedition to the eastern
end of Lake Ontario to punish the Senecas. Provisions ran
low and fever broke out. After reaching the La Famine (Sal-
mon) River he was forced by the Iroquois to sign a humili-
ating peace, abandoning France's western Indian allies to the
vengeance of the Iroquois. De la Barre was recalled to
France and replaced by the Sieur de Denonville.

1685    A French church, which maintained a separate identity until 1748, was founded in Boston.

The Sieur de Denonville arrived at Québec as the new governor.

A French admiral landed the Sieur de la Salle to the west of
the mouth of the Mississippi River. La Salle camped in Ma-
tagorda Bay, Texas, where he constructed Ft. St. Louis on
the La Vaca River for the first European settlers in Texas.

October. France revoked the Edict of Nantes which had
guaranteed Huguenot rights in France. This led to the second great wave of Huguenot migration to the United States,
with about 15,000 arriving between 1685 and 1750. Most of
the Huguenots settled in South Carolina, but large numbers
also landed in Pennsylvania, Virgina, New York, Rhode Island,
and Massachusetts. Though small in number, they wielded
a considerable influence because most were merchants, pro-
fessionals, and craftsmen. One of the new immigrants was
Pierre Jay, great-grandfather of John Jay. Others included
ancestors of the Faneuil, De Lancey, Boudinot, Bowdoin, and
Bernon families. (See document, page 129).

1686    France established an outpost at the mouth of the Arkansas
River.

Fifty Huguenot families settled at Frenchtown, Rhode Island.

Henry Collier, ancestor of the famous American family by
that name, arrived in the United States.

June 17. Étienne de Lancey, a native of Caen, arrived in New
York. An ancestor of the famous New York De Lanceys,
Étienne de Lancey became a leading merchant and donated
the first town clock set up in New York and the first fire en-
gine imported into the United States.

August. Fifteen French families arrived in New England,
with another shipload arriving in Salem the following month.
Some continued on to New York, Delaware, and South Carolina, but many remained, including the Cazneau, Sigourney,
Freneau, and Allaire families.

1687        About thirty Huguenot families settled at Oxford, Massachu-
            setts, on a 2,500-acre land grant. The settlement, located
            on the Manexit, or French River, existed as a buffer between
            Massachusetts and the Indians until after the Deerfield Mas-
            sacre of 1704. Led by Gabriel Bernon, Daniel Boudet and
            Isaac Bertrand du Tuffeau, the colony contained a French
            church and a number of 150-acre farms. Today a memorial
            marks the spot with the following inscription: "In Memory
            of the Huguenots, Exiles for Their Faith, Who Made the
            First Settlement of Oxford, 1687. 'We Live Not for Our-
            selves Only But For Posterity.'"

            Construction of a Huguenot church was begun in Charleston,
            South Carolina. The six other Huguenot settlements in South
            Carolina were located at Goose Creek, Orange Quarter,
            French Santee, Saint John's Berkeley, Purysburg, and New
            Bordeaux.

            March. The Sieur de la Salle gave up hope of rediscovering
            the mouth of the Mississippi River. He led his men north
            in an attempt to reach the Great Lakes, but was assassin-
            ated in Texas by mutineers under Duhaut.

            July. The governor of New France, the Marquis de Denon-
            ville, led 800 regulars, 800 colonials, and large numbers of
            Indian allies in an invasion of the Seneca territories, south
            of Lake Ontario. He destroyed four villages, burning all
            that he could not carry off, and constructed a small fort with
            a 100-man garrison at Niagara. While the Seneca were
            badly hurt, the invasion only stimulated the other Iroquois
            nations to increase their raids on French settlements dur-
            ing the following winter.

1688        An estimated 200 Huguenot families residing in New York
            comprised about 25 percent of the population of that city.

            Most of the 100-man garrison that the Marquis de Denon-
            ville left at Niagara in 1687 died during the winter. On Good
            Friday, 1688, Pierre Millet, a Jesuit priest, erected a
            cross and asked God's mercy for the plague-stricken garri-

son. Today a cross and plaque mark the spot, which was declared a national monument by President Calvin Coolidge
in 1925.

David Bonrepos founded a colony on Staten Island. In 1689
he moved to 6,000 acres of land purchased by Jacob Leisler,
a Dutch merchant, and founded New Rochelle. By 1694 there
were over twenty families residing in this village where the
American "rag carpet" was invented. By 1727 the population
reached 400. Michael Houdin, the last French pastor, died
in 1766. Among the many illustrious Americans to receive
an education in its fine schools were John Jay, Philip Schuy-
ler, Washington Irving, and Gouverneur Morris.

1689        Jean Cottin became the first schoolmaster at New Paltz,
            New York.

            Louis XIV reappointed the Comte de Frontenac as governor
            in New France.

            King William's War began in North America as an outgrowth
            of the War of the League of Augsburg in Europe.

            August 5. A force of 1,500 Iroquois razed the French settle-
            ment at Lachine on Montréal Island, killing 200 and abduct-
            ing another 90 people. An area of 7 1/2 miles along the St.
            Lawrence was devastated. Denonville's regulars were un-
            able to overtake the Indian warriors.

1690        January. Some 200 French and a large number of Indians
            left Montréal to attack the English settlements. At Schenec-
            tady they indiscriminantly killed 60 men, women and chil-
            dren, carrying many others into captivity.

            February. A party of French from Trois Rivières captured
            the English settlement at Salmon Falls. After uniting with
            a party from Québec, they then besieged and captured Ft.
            Loyal (Portland, Maine).

            May. Sir William Phips, with a force of New England coloni-
            als, captured the French post at Port Royal.

            October. John Schuyler led 140 English and Indians in an at-
            tack on La Prairie which killed or captured 24 people.

            October 15. Sir William Phips arrived at Québec, but the

French commander bluffed him into inactivity until reinforcements arrived to defend the city.

October 18. Le Règiment de Carignan, together with French
militia units, 1,500 strong, arrived from Montréal to save
Quebec from Phips's English force.

1691          French forces recaptured Port Royal from the English.

In a wave of anti-French feelings promoted by King William's War, a mob attacked and destroyed the Huguenot settlement at Frenchtown, Rhode Island.  Many Huguenots
were also arrested in Pennsylvania.

1692          In New York City the French population was second only in
number to that of the Dutch colonists.

At tiny Ft. Verchères, Madeleine de Verchères, age fourteen,
her two brothers, age ten and twelve, and three men held
off over fifty Iroquois for a week until Lt. de la Monnerie
arrived with forty men from Montréal.

1693          Huguenots in South Carolina were discriminated against as
"foreigners." They were, among other things, threatened with
loss of their estates upon their deaths.

The earliest description of a buffalo hunt was penned by Father Louis Hennepin in Louisiana.

A French Calvinist church was constructed in Charleston,
South Carolina.

A large force of Iroquois were defeated in an assault along
the St. Joseph River by French troops under Augustin le
Gardeur de Repentigny de Courtemanche.

1694          Governor Frontenac dispatched Antoine de la Mothe, Sieur
de Cadillac, as the new commandant in the west.

1695          The Sieur de Juchereau began the first industry on the Mississippi, a tannery at the confluence of the Ohio and Mississippi Rivers.

Pierre le Sueur concluded a peace between the Sioux and
Chippewa.

1696            Le Moyne d'Iberville raided Pemaquid and Placentia.

              May 21. Due to the flourishing fur trade, representatives
              of the king in New France reported a ten year supply of furs
              on hand. Because of this a royal ordinance revoked all fur
              trading licenses and prohibited colonials from carrying any
              goods to the western lands. Punishment for transgression
              was to be slavery in the galleys. This decree nearly des-
              troyed the economic viability of western New France.

1697            Le Moyne d'Iberville, commanding four warships and his
              own flagship, Le Pélican, defeated three British ships in
              Hudson's Bay, sinking the Hampshire. He then forced Gov-
              ernor Bailey to surrender Ft. Nelson.

              September 30. The Treaty of Ryswick ended King William's
              War with both sides returning to the status quo in the New
              World as it had been before the war. France re-occupied
              Acadia and England regained her foothold on Hudson's Bay.

1698            Between 1698 and 1702 Governor de Callières, carrying out
              the plans of Frontenac, signed peace agreements with the
              Iroquois. Because of this a lively rivalry developed for the
              western fur trade, and the New York frontier remained re-
              latively calm during Queen Anne's War, 1702-13.

              November. The Comte de Frontenac died, and was succeeded
              by Louis Hector, Comte de Callières.

1699            There were 438 French refugees in and about Charleston,
              South Carolina.

              April 8. Pierre le Moyne, Sieur d'Iberville, established Ft.
              Maurepas on the shores of Biloxi Bay. It was the first Euro-
              pean settlement in Mississippi. He later established a fort
              eighteen miles up the Mississippi, the first settlement in
              Louisiana. Two lakes discovered on the expedition were
              named for the two ministers under whose auspices the voy-
              age was made, Maurepas and Pontchartrain.

              June 29. The Sieur d'Iberville sent a report of his discover-
              ies to Jérôme de Pontchartrain, who impressed Louis XIV
              with the economic advantages to be gained by a second expe-
              dition to Louisiana.

              André Pénicaut, a companion of the Sieur d'Iberville, penned

<u>Annals</u> <u>of</u> <u>Louisiana,</u> describing his travels between 1699 and 1722.

The French established a post at Cahokia.

1700      A French post was established at Mackinac.

The Sieur de Bienville, in a report to Paris, first mentioned planting stalks of sugar cane at modern New Orleans.

By 1700 French fur traders achieved a virtual monopoly on the western areas. Their grip on the west was protected by forts at Frontenac, Detroit, Niagara, Sault Ste. Marie, Michilimackinac, Green Bay, St. Antoine, St. Nicholas, St. Croix, Perrot, and St. Louis.

Seven hundred Huguenots arrived in Virginia under the Marquis de la Muce and Charles de Sailly. The settlers were given 10,000 acres of land along the James River, twenty miles north of Richmond. Because the land was once owned by the Manakin Indians, the settlement was named Manakintown.

January 8. Le Moyne d'Iberville's second voyage to the Gulf Coast arrived at Biloxi Bay. He explored Louisiana for some five months, until he met a party of English under Captain Lewis Banks, who promised to return with a larger force to claim the area for William III. Iberville constructed Ft. de la Boulaye near the mouth of the Mississippi before returning to France.

September 8. Governor de Callières signed a treaty of peace between the Iroquois, Huron, Ottawa and Abenaki Nations.

1701      Antoine de la Mothe, Sieur de Cadillac, with 100 men from Lachine, built a small picket fort named Pontchartrain along the west bank of the river connecting Lakes Erie and Huron. The French term for the narrows at this point was <u>de</u> <u>troit</u>, hence the founding of modern Detroit.

October. Despite Spanish and English warnings, le Moyne d'Iberville left France for a third expedition to the Gulf of Mexico. Jérôme Phélypeaux, Comte de Pontchartrain, the Minister of Marine, ordered Iberville to establish a fortified outpost on Mobile Bay. To aid in founding the post, Pontchartrain sent with Iberville, Nicolas de la Salle, as supervisor of finance and police.

December 17. Le Moyne d'Iberville ordered the French colony at Biloxi transferred to Dauphin Island at Mobile.

1702        Queen Anne's War began as an outgrowth of the War of Spanish Succession in Europe. The period from 1702 to 1707 was characterized by the renewal of deadly border warfare, while large armies and coordinated expeditions marked the latter stages of the war, 1707-13.

1703        August. The Sieur de Beaubassin, with 500 French and Indians, attacked the English border towns in Maine. Their destruction left the Connecticut Valley open to French attacks.

1704        A British raid into Acadia ravaged the French settlements there, but was not strong enough to attack the garrison at Port Royal.

February 28-29. Major Hertel de Rouville led over 300 French and Indians in an attack on Deerfield, Massachusetts. The settlement was burned, 48 people were killed, and about 110 prisoners led away to Canada.

August 31. A census at Ft. Louis on the Mobile River, listed 180 soldiers, 27 families, 4 clergy, and a number of slaves.

1705        André Fresneau, grandfather of Philip Freneau, the "Laureate of the Revolution," arrived in Boston.

1706        July. Jean Baptiste le Moyne de Bienville became governor of lower Louisiana on the death of his brother, le Moyne d'Iberville.

A French-Spanish fleet arrived off Charleston, South Carolina, but delays alerted the defensive forces and the invaders retired after several small skirmishes.

August 1. A census at Ft. Louis on the Mobile River listed eighty-two heads of families.

1707        May. Colonel John March arrived in Acadia with 1,000 Massachusetts colonials. Subercase, the French commander, held his ground with only one-third as many men.

August. The English made a second attempt to take Acadia, but were again thwarted by a determined defense.

1708    Jean Baptiste le Moyne, Sieur de Bienville, constructed a
fort to protect the French settlers on Dauphin Island, on
the Gulf Coast.

A census at Ft. Louis on the Mobile River listed a garrison
of 122 plus 157 settlers.

1709    Mme. Ferree led the establishment of a Huguenot settlement
in Lancaster County, Pennsylvania.

The "Brandy Parliament" decided, against the strong protests of Bishop Laval, that brandy was needed in the fur
trade to rival Dutch gin and English rum.

Sir Francis Nicholson, with 1,500 men from the northern
English colonies, marched to the southern end of Lake Champlain, but his plan to attack Québec was given up when continental difficulties made British aid unavailable.

1710    The first English regulars landed in the New World to aid
in the colonial attack on Acadia. In order to avoid hopeless
bloodshed, Subercase surrendered Port Royal with the hon-
ors of war. In British hands, Port Royal became Annapolis
Royal, and the fall of Acadia marked the beginning of the
English conquest of New France.

Due to questionable practices in office, Bienville was replaced as governor in Louisiana by Antoine de la Mothe,
Sieur de Cadillac. Antoine Crozat, a Paris banker, appointed
as financial administrator, ran the colony strictly as a business enterprise. Louisiana did not emerge as a venture in
French imperialism until 1717.

September 9. English privateers from Jamaica plundered
the French settlements on Dauphin Island, torturing the inhabitants in search of information about mythical mines
they were supposed to be operating.

1712    Louis XIV ended military rule in Louisiana by establishing
a charter and a constitution. The Superior Council, including the governor, commissioner, attorney-general, and
several councilors appointed from the leading citizens, was
created to govern the colony.

1713    March 31. The Treaty of Utrecht ended Queen Anne's War.
Under the terms of the treaty equal trading rights were

granted to both French and English forces in North America.
France was forced to cede Newfoundland, Acadia, and Hudson's Bay to England, and to acknowledge a British protectorate over the Iroquois. Though a serious blow to the French empire, the alert negotiations of Jérôme Phélypeaux, Comte de Pontchartrain, preserved French presence in North America for another fifty years.

1714       Juchereau de St. Denis established Ft. St. Jean Baptiste at Natchitoches.

French engineers began the construction of the fortress at Louisbourg to prevent further English transgressions in New France.

1715       Louis XV succeeded to the French throne at the age of five.

August. The military strength of French Louisiana consisted of four companies, 160 men. The French Council of Marine attempted a reinforcement, but no troops could be found to send.

1716       Benard de le Harpe explored the Arkansas River, 1716-17.

The population of Canada reached 20,531.

1717       Ft. la Baye was erected, beginning the reentry of France into the Old Northwest after the 1698 edict of evacuation.

American merchants were admitted into the lucrative rum trade with the French West Indies. French molasses was cheap and New England distilleries were efficient, thus providing the backbone of New England commerce in the following years.

August. A royal decree established the Company of the West, which became the Company of the Indies after 1719. Antoine Crozat relinquished Louisiana to the Company.

September 20. Jean Baptiste le Moyne, Sieur de Bienville, was commissioned as commandant-general of Louisiana. Bienville sent his brother, Antoine le Moyne, Sieur de Chateaugué, to construct a fort at St. Joseph's Bay, east of Pensacola.

October 1. Sieur Arnaud Bonnaud was appointed warehouse keeper at New Orleans, thus beginning the permanent settlement of that area.

1718    The first cotton plantation in Louisiana was begun by Emanuel Prudhomme near Natchitoches.

√ The "Sieurs de Gentilly," Mathurin and Pierre Dreux, arrived in New Orleans and laid out their famous plantation Gentilly Terrace.

February. New Orleans, named for Philip of Orleans, was officially founded by the Sieur de Bienville, with fifty colonists.

April 14. Sieur Périer was sent to Louisiana as a colonial engineer. He died enroute and was replaced by le Blond de la Tour, who was aided by Sieur de Pauger, Sieur de Boispinel, and Franquet de Chaville.

May. Jean Beranger drew up the plans for Ft. Crèvecoeur, manned by a garrison of fifty.

June. Bienville, after protests by Spanish governor Juan Pedro Matamoros de Isla at Pensacola, ordered the destruction of Ft. Crèvecoeur.

A large number of colonists arrived in the Mississippi area, including 151 at Natchez, 82 on the Yazoo River, and 68 at New Orleans.

August. Three ships brought 800 colonists to Louisiana, among them the colony's first historian, le Page du Pratz. About 100 continued on to the Illinois country, with the remainder settling in Mississippi, Bay St. Louis, Biloxi, and Mobile.

1719    Fraunces Tavern, in New York City, where Washington delivered his Farewell Address in 1783, was built as a residential building.

January 9. France declared war on Spain.

April 19. Joseph le Moyne, Sieur de Sérigny, arrived at Dauphin Island with two ships loaded with armaments, soldiers, and settlers.

May 17. The Spanish governor, Matamoros de Isla, surrendered Pensacola to the Sieur de Bienville.

August 7. The Sieur de Chateaugué, with 250 troops and 42 noncombatants, surrendered Pensacola to a force of 1,200 Spanish troops under Governor Matamoros de Isla.

August 13. A Spanish force besieged Dauphin Island, but gave up the attempt on August 25.

September 17. Governor Matamoros de Isla surrendered Pensacola to the French with 1,800 prisoners and twelve vessels.

1720        Major Pierre Dugue Boisbriant, with 100 men, built Ft. Chartres sixteen miles from Kaskaskia.

France built Ft. Ouiatanon on the Wabash River west of modern Lafayette, Indiana.

Sebastian Râle, an anti-British Jesuit, incited Indian raids on the Maine frontier. England sent troops to the Kennebec and Penobscot rivers who destroyed French missions, killed Râle, and destroyed the power of the Abenakis.

1721        Adrien de Pauger laid out the plans for Old New Orleans, the "Vieux Carré, " as a fortified camp.

The Jesuit college at Kaskaskia, Illinois, was one of the first institutions of learning in the American Middle West.

The population of New Orleans reached 6,000 people, including 600 blacks.

Phillipe François Renault brought 200 miners and 500 slaves to work the mines he hoped to open near Ft. Chartres, close to Kaskaskia.

1722        The Sieur de Bienville brought the Capuchin friars to New Orleans. They established parish schools for boys.

The first permanent, large-scale planting of indigo in Louisiana began. The commercial manufacture of dye was begun by Nicholas de Beaubois, a Jesuit priest.

1723        About 20 percent of the population of Charleston, South Carolina was of French origin.

French officers at Ft. Chartres granted Phillipe François Renault permission to operate lead mines in Missouri.

1724    Veniard de Bourgmond explored the Nebraska, Kansas, and Osage rivers.

Father Cecil, a Capuchin, founded the first school for boys in New Orleans.

The Jesuits arrived in New Orleans.

England erected a post at Oswego, New York, in an attempt to lure the trade of the upper Great Lakes away from New France.

1725    April 17. William Mellichamp began the first salt concern in South Carolina and in the lower South.

1726    The population of Louisiana included 1,952 masters of households, 276 hired men and servants, 1,540 black slaves, and 229 Indian slaves.

Louis Thomas de Joncaire, Sieur de Chabert, obtained permission from the Iroquois to build a stone trading post at Niagara. Under Vaudreuil, the royal governor, and de Léry, the king's chief engineer in Canada, it became a complete fortress that counterbalanced the influence of the English post at Oswego. Built as a chateau to deceive the Indians, it was later strengthened by the engineer François Pouchot, and stands today as the only existing French castle in the United States.

1727    Captain John Gascoigne surveyed the South Carolina coast in the Alborough to make commerce safer.

Charles de la Boische, Marquis de Beauharnois, arrived in New France to replace Vaudreuil as governor. The period of Beauharnois's rule, 1727-48, marked the most prosperous years of the colony of New France.

August 7. Father Beaubois, superior of the Jesuits in Louisiana, persuaded the Ursuline nuns to open a convent in New Orleans. Nine professed nuns, 1 novice, and 2 postulates arrived on August 7, 1727. They immediately set up an academy for wealthy girls and a free day school. Later they opened a hospital and an orphanage. The curriculum in their schools included reading, writing, arithmetic, religion, and industrial training. Their impressive convent was designed by Broutin.

1728    A group of "filles à la cassette" (casket girls) arrived in Louisiana. The daughters of peasants or orphans of legitimate parents, they were cared for by the Ursuline nuns until they were married off. It was hoped that such shipments of willing young ladies would help ease the shortage of women in Louisiana.

Constant Marchand de Lignery led an expedition of 400 French and 800-900 Indians from Montréal against the hostile Fox Indians. At Mackinac they added another 300 Indians, but little was accomplished other than the torture of aged captives by the allied Indians.

1729    Old South Meeting House was constructed in Boston by master mason Joshua Blanchard, the same man responsible for constructing Faneuil Hall.

September 10. In a battle fought between the Illinois and Wabash rivers, a force of French and Indians under St. Ange, Villiers, Vincennes and des Noyelles, massacred about 500 Fox Indians and captured a like number. This was a severe blow to the power of the Fox Nation.

November 28. Hostile Indians massacred the French outpost at Ft. Rosalie near modern Natchez, Mississippi. The fort's commander, the Sieur de Chepart, was scalped and another 144 men, 35 women, and 56 children were killed. Tales of mutilation and torture had all of Louisiana in a panic.

1730    The convent of the Ursuline nuns, designed in the French style by Broutin, was constructed in New Orleans.

James de Lancey was appointed head of a commission to frame a charter for the city of New York. The resulting Montgomery Charter was primarily his work.

1731    The population of Louisiana numbered 5,000 Europeans and 2,000 blacks.

The Company of the Indies relinquished Louisiana to the control of Louis XV, making it once again a crown colony.

François Marie Bissot, Sieur de Vincennes, built a fort in Indiana where the city that bears his name still rests.

Pierre Gautier de Varennes, Sieur de la Vérendrye, with three sons and a nephew named la Jémerais, left Montréal to explore the western United States.

1732     John Peter Pury of Neuchâtel acquired 40,000 acres of land on the northwest bank of the Savannah River where 370 Swiss and French settled Purysburg, South Carolina. By 1734 the population grew to 600.

Jean Joseph Delfau de Pontalba arrived in New Orleans. Also established by this time were the families of Villeré, d'Arensbourg, de la Chaise, Chauvin, Huchet de Kernion, Lafrénière, de Livaudais, and Soniat du Fossat. Soon after Jean Étienne de Boré arrived.

1733     James de Lancey became chief justice of the New York Supreme Court.

Louis Denis, Sieur de la Ronde, and Jacques le Gardeur de St. Pierre, received permission to operate copper mines near Chequamegon Bay, Wisconsin.

In the early summer the Battle of Butte de Morts was fought between a force of French and warriors from the Sauk Nation in Wisconsin. Heavy losses were suffered by both sides, with the French losing many noteworthy leaders including Nicolas Coulon de Villiers, his son, Ailleboust, du Plessis, and le Gardeur. This battle, fought at Green Bay, resulted in the Sauk Nation abandoning the region and nearly amalgamating with the Fox Nation. The Fox and Sauk tribes then constructed a fort on the Wapsipinicon River in Iowa.

1734     The Ursuline nuns in New Orleans moved into their convent on Chartres Street.

A French punitive expedition under des Noyelles marched to the Fox and Sauk fort on the Wapsipinicon River in Iowa. The village was found abandoned. Several indecisive skirmishes were fought, with the French finally retreating due to hunger. French prestige was at its lowest ebb in the West.

1735     November. The first fire-insurance company in the United

States was established in Charleston, South Carolina. Huguenots were prominent among its organizers, and its first managers were Jacob Motte, James Crockett, and Henry Peronneau, Jr.

1736
The Huguenots in South Carolina founded a society to aid widows and orphans.

March 25. The Sieur de Bienville organized a punitive expedition against the Chickasaws, who were allied to the English in South Carolina. A group from Illinois under Pierre d'Artaguiette arrived at the rendezvous too early and was annihilated by the Indians. A few days later Bienville arrived, suffered heavy losses, and was pushed back to New Orleans. On Palm Sunday, March 25, the Chicasaw killed seventeen of their prisoners at the stake, including d'Artaguiette, Vincennes, Pierre St. Ange, the Jesuit chaplain Antoine Senat, and other French officers.

June 6. Jean de la Vérendrye, Father Aulneau and nineteen voyageurs were massacred by several hundred Sioux on an island near Ft. St. Charles.

1737
The chiefs of the western tribes arrived at Montréal to ask mercy for the Sauk and Fox Nations. Governor Beauharnois had no choice but to agree as French power in the West was minimal.

1738
Pierre de la Vérendrye explored western Minnesota, the Dakotas, and Manitoba. He opened a vast fur trade for New France and opened the way to the Pacific coast.

1739
The Mallet brothers explored the Nebraska area and named the Platte River. They reached as far as modern Taos and Santa Fé, New Mexico, in 1739-40.

The Sieur de Bienville moved north with French regulars under the Sieur de Noaille d'Aimé, provincials and Indians. The Chickasaws sued for peace upon this display of force.

War broke out between the Chippewa and Sioux Nations, with the French caught in the middle. La Ronde attempted to stop the hostilities, but was not successful and the Chippewa drove the Sioux out of central Wisconsin.

1740
By the 1740s shipyards had been established at Québec and ironworks near Trois Rivières.

Peter Faneuil, a wealthy Boston merchant, offered a public
market building as a gift to the city. The two-story brick
building, with a marketplace on the lower floor and a public
meeting hall on the upper, was accepted at a public meeting by a close vote of 367-360. Completed by French master
mason John Blanchard in 1742, the building burned in 1761,
but was reconstructed. Because of its extensive use by the
patriots prior to the American Revolution it has been called
the "Cradle of Liberty." It is still in use in Boston today.

King George's War began as the North American manifes-
tation of the War of Austrian Succession. It lasted until
1748.

1742          Jesuits in Louisiana imported from Santo Domingo large
quantities of sugar cane and skilled farm workers.

Jesuit scholar Father Meurin did valuable linguistic work
among Indians in the Illinois region.

September 10. The keys to the market of Faneuil Hall were
given to the city of Boston. (See 1740).

1743          The Sieur de Bienville resigned as governor of Louisiana.
He was succeeded by the Marquis de Vaudreuil, who changed
New Orleans from a drab military post to a center of "so-
ciety."

January 1. The three sons of la Vérendrye became the first
Frenchmen to view the Rocky Mountains in modern Wyoming.

September 30. The Chevalier François de la Vérendrye
buried a lead plate at Ft. Pierre, South Dakota. On it were
inscribed the names of the king, the Viceroy de Beauharnois,
Pierre Gauthier de la Vérendrye, his own name, and those
of his companions. The plaque was unearthed by school children in the twentieth century.

1744          Pierre François Xavier de Charlevoix, a Jesuit priest, published his Histoire de la Nouvelle France, which included
his earlier work, Journal historique. This descriptive account of his journey in Louisiana during the 1720s is the
only published account of the United States interior prior to
1750.

1745          The Illinois country, with a population of 900, sent 400,000
pounds of surplus grain to New Orleans.

May 3. The Royal Battery at Louisbourg fell to an invading English army, spelling the doom of the fortress.

June 16. Fortress Louisbourg fell to the English, opening the route to Québec via the St. Lawrence.

1746      A fleet under the Duc d'Anville sailed for New England to avenge the loss of Louisbourg, but it was defeated by disease and storms before seeing action.

1748      The Huguenot church in Boston dissolved.

October 18. The Treaty of Aix-la-Chappelle, which ended the War of Austrian Succession, returned Louisbourg to French control.

1749      French forces, between 1749 and 1753, constructed forts at Niagara and Venango, and pushed into the Ohio Valley.

June 15. Pierre Joseph Céleron, Sieur de Blainville, left Montréal with 20 regulars, 200 militia, and a few hundred Indians to assert French ownership to the Ohio Valley. Traveling south from Lake Erie, he buried, at intervals, leaden plates proclaiming the sovereignty of Louis XV. Roughly, his route carried him through Warren, Pennsylvania, Franklin and Wheeling, West Virginia, Marietta, Ohio, and Point Pleasant and Portsmouth, Ohio. (See document, page 131).

1750      An excellent example of French colonial architecture was Parlange built in Pointe Coupée Parish, Louisiana, by the Marquis de Tennant.

After the death of Chief Red Shoe in a battle with the French, the Choctaw Nation sued for peace.

The five French villages in the Illinois country included 1,100 Europeans, 300 blacks, and 60 Indians.

In the one-hundred-year period beginning in 1750 and ending in 1850, French political theorists helped popularize the idea of democracy in education to produce intelligent citizens and a free government.

1752      The Marquis du Quesne replaced Jonquière as governor-general of Canada. Du Quesne was determined to extend the area of French occupation and control.

1753        James de Lancey was appointed by the English crown as lieutenant-governor of New York. Due to frequent absences of the governor, de Lancey was the leading official in the colony a great deal of the time.

January. Governor Du Quesne sent Morin south to explore the French claims in the Ohio Valley.

June. Morin completed work on Ft. Presqu'Isle and established a 100-man garrison at the post. From there he proceeded to the Le Boeuf River (French Creek), where he constructed Ft. Le Boeuf.

1754        Pecaudy de Contrecoeur constructed Ft. Duquesne on the site of modern Pittsburgh.

The forty-seven planters in Louisiana were annually producing about 82,000 pounds of indigo.

May 28. The French and Indian War began when George Washington led a Virginia force in an attack on a French force under de Jumonville. Washington won the battle, fought near Uniontown, Pennsylvania, and de Jumonville was killed in the fighting. Washington hastily built Ft. Necessity for protection from the vengeful French.

June 19. James de Lancey presided over a convention of colonial leaders that met in New York to discuss the common defense against the Indians.

July 3. Coulon de Villiers, brother of the slain de Jumonville, led 800 French and Indians in an attack on Ft. Necessity, held by Washington with 350 men. Washington surrendered, leaving the Ohio Valley in control of France.

1755        The population of Canada numbered 55,009.

The English war fleet numbered 131 ships carrying 8,722 guns, while the French fleet numbered 71 vessels with 4,790 guns.

During the first full year of the French and Indian War the population of New France totaled less than 70,000. The English-speaking colonies contained 1,500,000 people.

Jean Gabriel Cerré established an important fur trading and merchant post at Kaskaskia, Illinois.

In what has been called "le Grand Dérangement, " over 6,000 Acadians were forced to leave Nova Scotia by the British government. Many of them died on voyages to new homes in Massachusetts, Maryland, and especially Louisiana. Most of the refugees settled in parishes along the Gulf Coast, west of New Orleans. Settling along Bayou Teche, in the vicinity of Lafayette, Louisiana, these settlers are known to this day as "Cajuns, " a corruption of "Acadians." The story of the massive migration provided the background for Henry Wadsworth Longfellow's Evangeline.

July 9. In the first major effort to reduce French power in the Ohio Valley area, General Braddock led 1,200 British and colonial troops, with eighteen guns, to capture Ft. Duquesne near modern Pittsburgh. The French commander, de Contrecoeur, knowning that Braddock's guns could easily reduce the fort, dispatched a force of 13 officers, 200 French and Canadians, 20 cadets, and 637 Indians to meet Braddock in the woods before the fort. Under the command of Captains de Ligneris, Dumas, and Beaujeu, the latter of whom was killed, the French force inflicted one of the worst defeats in the history of the Anglo-French rivalry in North America on Braddock's force. English losses included 63 of 86 officers, and nearly half of the 800 men actually engaged. General Braddock, who was mortally wounded, died on July 13.

1756

May 17. After nearly two years of hostility in North America, France and England formally declared war on each other. This began the Seven Years' War in Europe.

August 10. The Marquis de Montcalm, with 3,000 troops and fifty guns, attacked Ft. Ontario. The English defenders abandoned the works August 13, and fled to nearby Ft. Oswego.

August 14. Montcalm assaulted Ft. Oswego. The English commander was killed early in the bombardment, and the garrison of 1,200 surrendered after suffering just 5 casualties.

1757

January 11. Alexander Hamilton, of Huguenot ancestry, was born in the West Indies.

August 4. The Marquis de Montcalm besieged Ft. William
Henry, on Lake George, with an army of 8,000 men. Lt. Colonel Munro, with 2,140 defenders, held out five days before
surrendering on August 9. After the surrender the Indians
with Montcalm tomahawked about 50 of the English captives.
The slaughter was stopped by Montcalm and his regulars,
with great personal danger to the Marquis.

1758          Antoine Simon le Page du Pratz published his Histoire de la
              Louisiane.

              Joseph Dubreuil established the first large sugar plantation
              in Louisiana. The first shipload of low grade sugar was
              sent to France in 1765.

              March 13. About 200 Canadians and Indians, with a few
              French regulars dispatched by Colonel Hébécourt at Fort
              Carillon, met 180 of Rogers' Rangers at the Battle of Rogers'
              Rock near Lake George. Rogers's command suffered se-
              vere casualties.

              May. Brigadier General John Forbes led an English force
              toward Ft. Duquesne.

              June 2. Lord Jeffrey Amherst arrived at Louisbourg with
              forty warships and 12,000 regular troops. The French de-
              fenders numbered six warships, 3,000 regulars, 1,500 mi-
              litia, and 500 Indians under Drucour.

              July 8. The Marquis de Montcalm, with less than 4,000 troops
              from the regiments of La Sarre, Languedoc, La Reine, Guy-
              enne, Royal Rousillon, Bearn and Berry, was attacked at Ft.
              Carillon by 6,000 British regulars and 9,000 militia under
              General James Abercromby. In a disastrous assault on the
              French works, the British lost 1,600 regulars and 350 Pro-
              vincials, while Montcalm lost only 400 men.

              July 26. Louisbourg fell to the British, but Drucour held out
              long enough to prevent an attack on Québec.

              August 15. Lt. Colonel Bradstreet with 150 regulars and
              2,850 Provincials, left Ft. Stanwix to attack Ft. Frontenac,
              which contained only 155 defenders and 55 noncombatants.

              August 27. Fort Frontenac surrendered to the English. This
              cut French communications with the West and interrupted
              supplies bound for Ft. Duquesne.

September. A French force defeated a British advance party near Loyalhannon, Pennsylvania, killing 300 Highlanders and taking many prisoners.

November. France abandoned Ft. Duquesne in the face of superior numbers. General Forbes took possession of the destroyed fort and renamed it Pittsburgh.

1759    Michelson Godhart de Brules, a New York engraver from 1759 to 1763, became the first known French artist in the United States since the ill-fated Ribaut expedition.

July 26. The 500-man garrison of Ft. Niagara was surrendered by Prochot, after a commendable defense, to General John Prideaux with 2,200 British regulars, 2,800 Provincials, and 900 Iroquois under Sir William Johnson. The siege of Niagara lasted three weeks and ended only after the defeat of a force sent to relieve the garrison.

July 26. Bourlamanque, with 2,500 men, abandoned Ft. Carillon to 11,000 men under Lord Amherst. The fortress, much of which was destroyed by the retreating French, was called Ticonderoga by the British.

Crown Point was abandoned to the British.

Bourlamanque made a successful stand at Isle-aux-Noix that stopped Amherst's movement toward Montréal. The British fell back and wintered at Crown Point.

September 13. At the Battle of the Plains of Abraham, outside Québec, Montcalm's five French regiments were defeated by six British regiments under General Wolfe. Both of the commanding officers were killed in the fighting, which saw the English use the "thin red line" of two ranks for the first time. The defeat caused the surrender of Quebec and the virtual end of New France, but the real reason for the fall of the city was probably the corruptness and bungling of Vaudreuil and Bigot.

1760    Pierre Lorillard, an eighteen-year-old Huguenot from Montbeliard, France, founded P. Lorillard Company in New York City, a tobacco merchandising firm which is still in existence today.

April 28. In an attempt to retake Québec, Lévis sent 6,000

men from Montréal to attack the British under General Murray. Although the French inflicted severe losses on the British at the Battle of Sainte Foy, the British remained within the works at Québec and held out until reinforcements arrived.

September 8. New France expired with the surrender of Montréal.

November 29. Detroit was surrendered by Belêtre to Major Robert Rogers.

1762 May 28. A British Order in Council referred to 114 Huguenots who desired to settle in the British colonies in North America. Some 20,000 acres of land along the Savannah River were given to 212 settlers under Rev. Jean Louis Gilbert. The settlement, New Bordeaux, became famous for farming and silk manufacturing.

November. By the secret Treaty of Fontainebleau, France ceded to Spain all of her territory west of the Mississippi, as well as the Isle of Orleans in Louisiana. The news did not reach Louisiana until September, 1764.

1763 The Jesuits were expelled from Louisiana, but returned with its cession to Spain.

February 10. The Treaty of Paris, ending the Seven Years' War, ceded to England all of Canada and all French lands east of the Mississippi River except New Orleans. The treaty also gave to England the French islands in the West Indies and India, thus ending the French empire as a major factor in global politics.

October. Vermont officially acquired its name from the French words meaning "green mountain."

1764 Pierre la Clede founded St. Louis, constructed by René Auguste Chouteau.

Large numbers of French settled at New Bordeaux, South Carolina.

September. The incredulous population of Louisiana learned for the first time of their cession to Spain.

1765            Daniel Dulany published <u>Considerations</u> <u>on</u> <u>the</u> <u>Propriety</u> of
                <u>Imposing</u> <u>Taxes</u> <u>in</u> <u>the</u> <u>British</u> <u>Colonies,</u> which opposed the
                Stamp Act.

                Joseph Dubreuil exported the first large shipment of low
                grade sugar from Louisiana to France.

                October. John Bayard, a merchant who was one of the ori-
                ginal "Sons of Liberty, " became one of the first to sign the
                nonimportation agreement despite its adverse effects on
                his own business.

1766            The populations of French-settled areas were as follows:
                Kaskaskia, 600; Cahokia, 300; Illinois, 1, 000; Vincennes,
                300; Detroit, 600; and New Orleans, 1,800.

                Anthony Benezet published the first antislavery book in the
                United States, <u>A</u> <u>Caution</u> <u>and</u> <u>Warning</u> <u>to</u> <u>Great</u> <u>Britain</u> <u>and</u>
                <u>Her</u> <u>Colonies</u> <u>on</u> <u>the</u> <u>Calamitous</u> <u>State</u> <u>of</u> <u>the</u> <u>Enslaved</u> <u>Ne-</u>
                <u>groes</u>. Later in life he took up the crusade of the American
                Indians.

                March. Don Antonio de Ulloa arrived with two companies of
                Spanish infantry to take possession of Louisiana. French
                bitterness led to the ten-month Lafrénière Insurrection,
                making Louisiana the first American colony to rebel against
                a European power.

1768            A silver bowl moulded by Paul Revere was presented to
                ninety-two Massachusetts Representatives who resisted
                King George III's restrictive trade policies.

                October 29. The French in Louisiana began the first revolt
                against a European power when they defied Spanish Governor
                Ulloa in the Lafrénière Insurrection.

1769            August. Twenty-four ships carrying 2,000 troops under Don
                Alexandro O'Reilly left Spain to put down the rebellion in
                Louisiana.

                October 25. Five leaders of the Lafrénière Insurrection
                were executed. Others were given varying prison terms.

1770            March 5. Seven Boston citizens were killed by British troops,
                defending themselves from attack, in what colonial propagan-
                dists called the "Boston Massacre. " Anti-British hatreds

were stirred up by revolutionaries including Paul Revere,
of Huguenot descent, whose engraving of the event is probably his most famous work, if also one of his worst.

1774            Abram Markos (Marcou) of Philadelphia organized the company of light horse called the City Troop of Philadelphia,
of which he became captain.

Louis XVI took control of the reins of government in France,
with Charles Gravier, Comte de Vergennes, as his minister
of foreign affairs. Vergennes quickly perceived the latent
potential for revolt in North America and determined to use
it to French advantage.

March. Judge John Faucheraud Grimké, father of the famous
Abolitionist sisters from South Carolina, joined his name
to those of other prominent figures on a petition to "His
Brittanic Majesty" protesting the Boston Port Bill.

September 5. Rev. Jacob Duché opened the first Continental
Congress with a prayer. French descendants were very
prominent among its membership, including three who later
served as its president:  John Jay, Henry Laurens, and Elias
Boudinot.

September 11. Paul Revere left Milton, Massachusetts, for
Philadelphia with copies of the Suffolk Resolves for the Continental Congress. He arrived September 16, after traveling 319 miles through five states.

1775            James Bowdoin served as president of the Council of Twenty-
Eight, chosen to govern the Massachusetts Bay Province by
the revolutionaries.

Dr. Ephraim Brevard authored the North Carolina  Meck-
lenberg Declaration of independence.

April 18-19. Paul Revere rode to warn the Massachusetts
countryside of approaching British troops.

November. The Continental Congress authorized the first
American agents sent to France.

Pierre Augustin de Beaumarchais, a French dramatist and
adventurer, conversed with Arthur Lee about the possibility
of French aid to the United States. As a result of these ne-

gotiations the firm of Rodrigue Hortalez et Cie began selling merchandise to Timothy Jones of Bermuda. Jones was really Silas Deane, the American representative to France. Thus Beaumarchais became the first vendor of ammunition to the United States.

December 31. American General Richard Montgomery, of Huguenot descent, was killed in the American assault on Québec.

1776      John Jay was a leader in drawing up the New York constitution.

Pierre Chenet, nicknamed "Perique," introduced perique tobacco as a commercial crop in Louisiana. This was a strong variety of black tobacco usually mixed with milder strains.

The University of North Carolina was founded as a state university offering a secular education. The French plan of state education proved very influential in eighteenth-century America, with leading exponents including Benjamin Franklin, John Adams, Thomas Jefferson, John Jay, and Ezra L'Hommedieu. Jay and L'Hommedieu, both of French descent, originated the University of the State of New York in 1784. French education experts in the United States left a lasting impact on secular education.

March. The Comte de Vergennes, French foreign minister, was assured by Spain of cooperation against England.

May 2. Pierre Augustin de Beaumarchais received financial assistance from the French government to send secret aid to the United States. This aid included ammunition, clothing, and cannons.

June 10. The Continental Congress resolved "That it is expedient forthwith to take the most effectual measures for forming foreign alliances." The plan was aimed specifically at France.

August. The Comte de Vergennes urged Louis XVI to intervene in the American Revolution: "The war will form a connection between France and North America which will not be merely a temporary expedient. Nothing can divide the two nations. Commerce will form a durable if not eternal chain between them; it will revive industry, bringing into our harbors the commodities which America formerly poured into English ports."

September 26. The Continental Congress appointed a three-man commission to negotiate for an official treaty of alliance in Paris.

December. Benjamin Franklin, the most widely respected American in Europe, left for Paris on behalf of the Continental Congress.

The Declaration of Independence, issued in 1776, provided the inspiration for Asher Brown Durand's engraving of Trumbull's <u>Declaration</u> of <u>Independence</u>.

1777        The Marquis de Lafayette and Johann de Kalb arrived from France to fight for American independence. General Thomas Conway had also previously served in the French army.

Pierre Charles L'Enfant, the future architect of Washington, D.C., arrived in the United States to donate his engineering skills to the American cause. He later designed the insignia for the Society of the Cincinnati.

December 17. General Washington went into winter quarters at Valley Forge, designed by French engineer Louis L. Duportail.

December 17. After news arrived at Versailles detailing Burgoyne's surrender at Saratoga, France officially recognized American independence.

1778        John Jay, of Huguenot descent, was elected president of the Continental Congress.

Daniel Roberdeau established a lead mine in western Pennsylvania at his own expense to produce lead for the American army. He built Ft. Roberdeau to defend the works.

John Bayard was elected speaker of the Pennsylvania Assembly.

French engineers under the supervision of the Polish volunteer Tadeusz Kościuszko constructed the famous chain boom at West Point.

February 6. Benjamin Franklin, Silas Deane, and Arthur Lee, the American plenipotentiaries in Paris, affixed their signatures to a treaty that bound France to support the American movement for independence. Signing for France was Conrad Alexandre Gérard, Chevalier de Rayneval. It was the first treaty of alliance negotiated by the United States, and pledged France to supply the Americans with cannon, muskets, powder, and direct military intervention. France renounced all claims east of the Mississippi River, including Canada, and each side agreed not to sign a separate peace.

February 14. In Quiberon Bay, John Paul Jones, commanding the American ship Ranger, saluted the French flag. Admiral La Motte Picquet, commander of the French fleet, returned the salute. This was the first official recognition of the United States flag by any foreign power.

April 25. Charles Hector, Comte d'Estaing, sailed from Toulon with 4,000 French regulars, five frigates, and twelve ships-of-the-line, bound for the United States.

May 27. The Continental Congress authorized the establishment of an Engineering Department of three companies, organized mainly along the lines of the French Corps du Génie of Vauban. Led by the Polish volunteer Tadeusz Kościuszko, its subcommanders included Radière, du Portail, and du Cambray.

July. Conrad Alexandre Gerard was appointed ambassador to the United States by Louis XVI. He was the first foreign diplomatic representative credited to the United States.

July 4. George Rogers Clarke captured Kaskaskia and Cahokia. Father Gibault, the French priest in the area, convinced the defenders of Vincennes to surrender when he assured them that the French Alliance was a reality. The French settlers then aided Clarke in the conquest of the Northwest.

July 29. The Comte d'Estaing arrived off New York Harbor with a French fleet to aid the United States.

August 20. The French-American assault on Newport, Rhode Island, failed when a storm damaged the French fleet under the Comte d'Estaing.

November 4. The Comte d'Estaing left Boston Harbor for the West Indies. The first joint Franco-American action in North America thus ended in failure.

After the French Alliance was signed, French cookery became popular in the United States. French words that we use with great currency today began to appear in the English colonies. These included bouillon, consommé, purée, fricassee, mayonnaise, pâté, and hors d'oeuvres.

1779    A severe hurricane destroyed many French homes in New Orleans.

James Bowdoin was elected presiding officer of the Massachusetts Constitutional Convention.

Judge John Faucheraud Grimké published South Carolina Justice of the Peace and Duty of Executors and Administrators. His compilation of laws, Public Laws of the State of South Carolina served for several decades as the most important documentation of laws in the state.

January 11. The Marquis de Lafayette was sent to France to explain the failure of the operations with the Comte d'Estaing, and ask for a larger fleet and regular troops that would be under instructions more favorable to the American mentality. (See document, page 132).

July 26. Lt. Colonel François Louis Teisseidre de Fleury received the first decoration granted by the United States to a foreign national for his leadership of American forces at Stony Point, July 15, 1779.

September 4. Charles Hector, Comte d'Estaing, arrived off the Savannah River with thirty-seven French ships carrying over 2,000 guns and 6,000 regular troops.

September 12. The Comte d'Estaing landed 3,500 troops at Savannah and called on the British commander to surrender. British reinforcements arrived and the commander decided to hold out.

September 23. Off Flamborough Head, John Paul Jones attacked a British convoy. Sailing in a French ship renamed the Bonhomme Richard, and with the aid of the French ship Pallas, he attacked the British ships Serapis and Countess

of Scarborough. His victory over the Serapis was the first
major episode of heroics in American naval history.

October 2. The French and American armies besieging Savannah opened fire on the British.

October 9. The allied assault on Savannah failed. British
losses were 155, while combined French and American
casualties amounted to 837.

October 9-22. The allied armies under Sullivan and d'Estaing besieged Savannah. The attempt failed.

1780          Anthony Benezet was influencial in the decision of the Pennsylvania legislature to abolish slavery.

French became a regular subject of instruction at Harvard
University and the College of William and Mary.

French cooking, long present in the United States, gained
widespread popularity. After first adopting special forms
of buns and rolls, non-French colonists soon prepared the
"delicately flavored French soups, the light omelettes, the
delicious entrées" that are typical of French cuisine.

January. John Jay, of Huguenot descent, arrived in Spain as
American minister plenipotentiary. He succeeded in gaining material support from Spain.

March 1. At Versailles, Louis XVI signed the orders for
the French army being sent to the United States under Jean
Baptiste Donatien de Vimeur, Comte de Rochambeau. The
orders were to be opened in the mid-Atlantic. (See document, page 132).

July 11. The French army of the Comte de Rochambeau em-
barked, 6,000 strong, at Newport, Rhode Island. The army
was to operate as a unit, but under the command of General
Washington.

November 26. George Washington expressed his official
thanks to the Marquis de Lafayette in his General Orders.

1781          Duncan Phyfe arrived in the United States. He specialized
in the manufacture of French-style furniture that made his
name famous throughout the nation. He was of Scottish origin.

Elias Boudinot was elected president of the Continental Congress.

John Jay and Henry Laurens, both of Huguenot descent, were appointed, along with Adams, Jefferson and Franklin, to engage in peace negotiations with the English.

August. By August, 1781, Washington's Continental Army was bankrupt. The Comte de Rochambeau's war chest contained French livres worth 40,000 gold American dollars. Without question he gave half to Washington to finance the upcoming campaign that ended in the victory at Yorktown.

August 14. General Washington received word that François Joseph Paul, Comte de Grasse, would arrive in the Chesapeake Bay during September with a French fleet and 3,000 troops. With this information, Washington determined to try and defeat Lord Cornwallis's British army in Virginia.

August 16. The Comte de Rochambeau wrote to the minister of war in Versailles that he was marching south with Washington.

September 4. The French army passed through Philadelphia on its way south to Yorktown. The troops made a dramatic impression on both the citizenry and the Continental Congress. Thousands turned out for a drill performed by the Règiment de Soissonais.

September 5. The French fleet under the Comte de Grasse entered Chesapeake Bay and engaged the English fleet under Admiral Graves. De Grasse, with twenty-four ships, beat the British fleet of nineteen ships after a six-day action that caused Graves to retire to New York. This ended any hope of relieving the British army at Yorktown from the sea.

September 26. Washington's army concentrated around Williamsburg, Virginia. It numbered 3,800 Continentals under Washington, 2,500 Continentals under Lafayette, 4,000 French under Rochambeau, and 3,800 French from Martinique under the Marquis de Saint Simon. This number was increasing daily by the addition of Virginia militia under General Weedon.

October 19. General O'Hara, acting for Lord Cornwallis, surrendered 8,000 British troops at Yorktown to the Franco-American forces under Washington and Rochambeau.

1782
Michel Guillaume Jean de Crèvecoeur (Hector St. Jean de Crèvecoeur) published Letters from an American Farmer. It was an excellent description of American frontier life, economy, and society. He "pictured America as a land of plenty for men of every occupation and every social objective."

Columbia University appointed its first French professor, and Brown University sought the aid of Louis XVI in doing the same.

About 1782 Alexandre Marie Quesnay, Chevalier de Beaurepaire, presented in Philadelphia the first French dramatic production in the United States, Beaumarchais's Eugénie.

1783
Between 1775 and 1783 Jacques Donatien le Ray de Chaumont loaned the United States government 2 million francs, his entire fortune. This included outfitting ships for John Paul Jones.

During the American Revolution Gabriel Manigault loaned the American government 220,000 pounds sterling for the war effort.

April 19. George Washington selected Rev. John Gano, a descendant of the Ganeau family, to offer a prayer of thanks for the successful conclusion of peace with Great Britain.

May 10. The Order of the Cincinnati was established. Louis XVI became a patron, and the membership included Lafayette, Rochambeau, de Grasse, Chastellux, Dumas, de Noailles, Collot, Deux Ponts, Lauzun, Charles Alexandre, Theodore de Lameth, Bougainville, Ségur, Broglie, Custine, Ferson, Blanchard, du Bourg, Bozon de Périgord, Closen, Pontgibaud, Ternant, Gérard, and Luzerne.

September 3. The Treaty of Paris was formally signed, gaining independence for the United States. Signing as president of the Continental Congress was Elias Boudinot.

December 4. In Fraunces Tavern, formerly the home of Etienne de Lancey, Washington bade farewell to his officers.

1784
The Marquis de Lafayette visited the United States amid general rejoicing.

John Sevier was elected governor of the new state of Franklin, which existed for two years. He was later elected governor of Tennessee, serving three terms. After being out of office he was then reelected for another three terms.

June. Boinod and Gaillard published the first French newspaper in the United States in Philadelphia, Le Courrier de l'Amérique. No copies now exist because it was published for only a short time.

August 30. France closed her West Indian ports to the United States, but the new rules were not well enforced.

1785      John Jay became president of the New York antislavery society. It was largely through his efforts that New York abolished slavery in 1799.

Pierre Étienne du Ponceau was admitted to the bar. He later became the leading American expert on international law.

James Bowdoin was elected governor of Massachusetts. He was responsible for the swift government action during Shay's Rebellion.

1786      André Michaux, French botanist, was sent to Charleston, South Carolina, to establish a garden and send samples to Paris. He purchased lands ten miles up the neck between the Ashley and Cooper Rivers. Known as the French Botanic Garden, it introduced such Far Eastern flowers as the camellia, mimosa, crepe myrtle, and tea olive into the United States.

September 15. Jean François Galoup de la Pérouse anchored off Monterey, the first significant contact of the French with the Pacific Coast of North America. He sailed on the frigate Boussole and was accompanied by the Astrolabe under M. de Langle.

1787      The populations of French settlements along the Wabash and Illinois rivers were as follows: Vincennes, 520; Kaskaskia, 191; Cahokia, 239; St. Philippe, 239; Praire du Rocher, 78.

January. Crèvecoeur, Clavière and Brissot de Warville attempted to establish a Société Gallo-Américaine. It later merged with the Société des Amis de Noirs, organized in February, 1788. Backed primarily by French people, the membership included Mirabeau, Lafayette, La Rochefoucauld-

Liancourt, Sieyes, Gregoire, Volney, William Short, and Crevecoeur. It was an important organization devoted to the emancipation of blacks.

1788　　　Julien Dubuque became the first European settler in Iowa when he negotiated with the Fox Indians to work lead mines in the Iowa country.

Fire destroyed 856 homes in New Orleans, about half of the entire town.

Jean Antoine Houdon, a famous French sculptor, came to the United States to sculpt Washington's statue. His work, now in the state capitol at Richmond, Virginia, was pronounced by Lafayette to be "a facsimile of Washington's person."

The Miscellaneous Works of Freneau established Philip Freneau as one of America's greatest poets.

1789　　　Caffières, a sculptor of Louis XVI, executed a statue of General Richard Montgomery for the front of St. Paul's Church in New York City.

Henry Elouis, a noted miniaturist who studied under Restout, worked in Baltimore and Philadelphia in the years 1789-1807.

The French Revolution began, with widespread support in the United States.

The Society of the Scioto was organized in Paris to encourage French migration to lands in Pennsylvania. The company eventually sold some 10,000 acres to 600 French settlers.

September 2. Alexander Hamilton, of Huguenot descent, was named the first secretary of the treasury. Elias Boudinot was named director of the mint in 1795, and Michael Hilligas became the first treasurer of the United States.

September 26. John Jay was appointed first chief justice of the Supreme Court.

1790　　　During 1789-90 the Scioto Company offered in Paris, at six livres per acre, land probably not worth much more than six or seven sous an acre. The first shipload of 200 French arrived in Alexandria, Virginia, in May, 1790. Located on the Ohio River, near modern Gallipolis, Ohio, the colony was founded by Rebel d'Eprémesnil. It was beset by lack of proper housing, dishonesty of the Paris agent who absconded with the company funds, malarial mosquitoes, defective land titles, and hostile Indians. By 1792 the colony had failed, ending the hopes of large-scale immigration promoted by speculators in Paris.

The United States census listed 54,900 French natives in the United States.

During the 1790s French emigres made lasting contributions to American Catholicism. They increased substantially the number of American Catholics, the influx of French priests relieved the shortage of Catholic clergy, and ultimately these émigrés exercised an important influence on the American Catholic hierarchy.

Between 1790 and 1800 French refugees flocked to the United States. Estimates on the number of those who arrived in the United States vary from 10,000 to 25,000.

During the decade of the 1790s French refugee colonies were established on the Black River in northern New York, at Greene on the Chenango River in New York, on the Susquehanna River at Azilum, and at Fontaine Leval in Maine.

Charles le Boulanger de Boisfremont completed, between 1790 and 1800, fourteen portraits of American Revolutionary figures begun by Peale.

Jean Pierre Bauduy became famous as an oil painter and through designing Wilmington's city hall. He worked in the E.I. du Pont gunpowder works, and brought the first merino sheep into the United States.

Before the era of the camera, Saint Mémin completed about 800 etchings of famous Americans.

Louis François de Paul Binose de Saint Victor began painting miniatures. He was the grandfather of the famous American artist John La Farge.

In Baltimore, the architect Godefroi designed the Gothic chapel of St. Mary's College, the Unitarian Church, and, in conjunction with Latrobe, the stock exchange building.

Jean Deveze, an émigré doctor, replaced bleeding with the use of stimulants and quinine to treat yellow fever.

Refugees from Santo Domingo began the newspaper Le Patriote Français in Charleston, South Carolina.

Moses Austin, father of the founder of Austin, Texas, lived in the French colony of Ste. Genevieve along the Mississippi River.

Peter Fayssoux became the first president of the South Carolina Medical Society.

A French company in Baltimore performed Pergolesi's opera La Serva Padrona.

The architecture of the Roman revival became popular in the United States when Thomas Jefferson planned the Virginia state capitol at Richmond along the lines of the Maison Caree at Nîmes, France.

Enthusiasm among the American populace ran high in favor of the French Revolution. Thomas Jefferson led the pro-French Republicans, who began erecting Liberty Poles. French manners became popular, clubs were formed along the lines of the Paris Jacobins, and members of secret societies addressed each other as "Citizen."

Edmond Charles Genêt arrived in Charleston, South Carolina, as the new French ambassador to the United States. Genêt annoyed his friends by shunning diplomatic courtesy, commissioning privateers, inciting Americans against the Spanish in Florida, and even appealing to the American people to violate President Washington's proclamation of neutrality. The problem ended with France recalling Genêt after American protests. Afraid to return to the vengeance of the Jacobins, Genêt was granted political asylum in the United States.

1791        The Théâtre de St. Pierre opened in New Orleans, making that city the center of American operatic performances until the Civil War.

Philip Freneau, a famous poet, began editing the National Gazette, founded in 1791 to support the Republican philosophies of Thomas Jefferson. This led directly to the rise of political parties in the United States.

Francis Dana became chief justice of the Massachusetts Supreme Court, a position he held for fifteen years.

Pierre Charles l'Enfant laid out the original plan of Washington, D.C., based in part on the garden plan of the great palace of Versailles.

Father Francis Charles Nagot founded St. Mary's Seminary at Baltimore with three Sulpician instructors and five seminarians.

A special act of Congress provided 400 acres of land to each head of a family who made improvements on lands in Illinois prior to 1788. Of 244 titles granted, 164 went to French inhabitants of that area.

Between 1791 and 1799, twenty-four French priests arrived in the United States. Six later became bishops.

Congress granted 24,000 acres, known as the French Grant, to refugees in Scioto County, but most of the dissatisfied colonists left anyway.

The first company of French actors arrived in Louisiana.

A black revolt in Santo Domingo sent between 10,000 and 20,000 French fleeing to the United States between 1791 and 1793.

1792        Large numbers of refugees from Santo Domingo landed in Philadelphia, New York, Baltimore, Charleston, and Louisiana.

François Alexandre Frédéric, Duc de la Rouchefoucald-Liancourt, arrived in Philadelphia. He left a vivid, realistic portrayal of the United States, including important scientific and travel accounts.

January. M. Placide, a rope dancer, performed on stage in Charleston, South Carolina. His appearance triggered a great vogue of French jugglers, sword-swallowers and trick dancers on the American stage.

August 31. William Constable sold M. Paul Chassanis 630,000 acres of land north and east of the Black River in northern New York. Chassanis formed La Compagnie de

New York to sell bonds, at a profit, to refugees of the
French Revolution for a Royalist colony. (See document,
page 136).

September 21. The French Republic was proclaimed, gaining strong support in the United States.

1793      Brillat Savarin, a refugee of the French Revolution, introduced the gastronomic delights of the cheese omelette to
the United States.

During a yellow fever epidemic in Philadelphia, Stephen Girard was instrumental in organizing hospitals for those
stricken.

January 9. J.P.F. Blanchard made the first successful bal-
loon flight in the United States at Philadelphia.

January 21. As the Reign of Terror began in France, the
Revolution lost much of its American support.

February 1. The war between England and France began.
Many pro-French British moved to the United States, including Joseph Priestly and Thomas Cooper.

Spring. Louis Marie, Vicomte de Noailles, and Antoine
Omer Talon purchased lands for the Royalist colony of Azilum in Pennsylvania.

May 18. President Washington received Ambassador Genêt,
initiating a policy of de facto recognition for the French Republic.

May 25. Father Stephen Badin became the first Catholic
priest ordained in the United States.

June 28. M. Paul Chassanis, in Paris, drew up the prospectus for the new Castorland Company. Coins were minted
containing about fifty cents' worth of silver apiece to pay
the commissioners. Some of these "Castorland Half-dollars"
are still extant in collections. (See document, page 136).

1794      Samuel Bayard served as the government prosecuting agent
in the placing of claims before the British Court of Admi-
ralty. He later became instrumental in founding the New
York Historical Society.

Louis Duclot, a Santo Domingo refugee, established the first Louisiana newspaper, Le Moniteur de la Louisiane.

Congress appropriated $15,000 against the debt of France for relief of the Santo Domingo exiles.

One of the few French attempts to establish a rural community began when a small number of émigrés and Santo Domingo Creoles left Philadelphia to establish a Royalist settlement at Azilum on the Susquehanna River. Led by de Noailles and Talon, the backers hoped to buy up a million acres of land at fifteen cents per acre and resell it at three dollars per acre. The proceeds would go toward developing the colony.

April 10. The French theater opened in Charleston, South Carolina, presenting a "democratic" form of entertainment including harlequins, clowns, and the famous rope walker Alexander Placide.

November 11. Jean Baptiste Trudeau established the first settlement in the Dakotas.

November 19. The Jay Treaty was signed in England. Soundly criticized in the United States, the treaty was condemned in France and proved to be a turning point in Franco-American relations.

Bowdoin College, named for its Huguenot benefactor, was incorporated in Brunswick, Maine.

1795          Jean Louis Lefebvre de Cheverus, the future bishop of Boston, arrived in the United States.

Anne Louis de Tousard joined the U.S. Army. He supervised the building of fortifications at West Point and Newport, Rhode Island.

Elias Boudinot became director of the U.S. Mint and Michael Hilligas, another Huguenot descendant, became first treasurer of the United States.

Étienne de Boré harvested the first commercial sugar crop in Louisiana, making the huge sum of $12,000. He successfully refined the sugar, thus beginning the American sugar industry.

In the belief that there was universal public opposition to the Jay Treaty in the United States, France sent Pierre Auguste Adet to stir these feelings into action. Adet lobbied in the House, the Senate, and with the president, but with no success. He then threw his resources into supporting pro-French Republicans against British-oriented Federalists in the election of 1796.

1796

The Pennsylvania and Massachusetts legislatures granted funds to aid destitute French refugees. Philadelphia raised $14,500, Baltimore contributed $12,000, Portsmouth, Hampton and Williamsburg raised over $10,000, and New York City provided $11,000, a sum matched by the state legislature.

M. Demilliere became a famous painter of miniatures in New York.

France, angry at the Jay Treaty, seized over 300 American ships in one year and refused to receive Charles C. Pinckney as the American minister.

Physician Felix Pascalis-Ouvriere wrote important accounts of yellow fever outbreaks in Philadelphia in 1796 and 1798.

Louis Philippe, future king of France, spent 1796-99 in a small room over a saloon in Philadelphia.

1797

Three sons of the Duc d'Orleans visited the Azilum colony. They were the Duc d'Orleans, Duc de Montpensier, and Comte de Beaujolais.

May 31. C.C. Pinckney, John Marshall, and Elbridge Gerry were appointed to secure a commercial treaty with France. They were received informally by Talleyrand, but were later approached by three men who suggested a gift of 1,200,000 francs to improve negotiations. Pinckney refused their suggestion and referred to them as "X. Y. and Z." in his report of the incident. Talleyrand protested no knowledge of the three, but the "XYZ Affair" strained Franco-American relations. (See document, page 141).

1798

The legislation allowing Frenchmen to own land in New York State was rescinded, thus making the titles sold by the Castorland Company invalid.

The "XYZ Affair" led to a wave of xenophobia and directly
to the passage, by a Federalist Congress, of the Alien and
Sedition Acts. This caused many apprehensive French emigres to leave the country.

Benjamin H. Latrobe wrote the first pamphlet advocating
the establishment of permanent city water supplies.

Paul Joseph Nancrede published the French newspaper Cour-
ier de Boston. He had also published the first French gram-
mar for use in American colleges, L'Abeille Françoise.

After France had seized nearly 1,000 American vessels,
an undeclared naval war broke out between France and the
United States.

February 9. Near St. Kitts in the West Indies the USS Con-
stellation, with thirty-eight guns, defeated the forty-gun
French ship l'Insurgente in the first action of the undeclared
naval war between the two nations.

July 14. The United States abrogated its treaty with France.

1799        Pierre Samuel du Pont de Nemours arrived in the United
            States. His son founded E.I. du Pont de Nemours and Com-
            pany.

1800        During the first two decades of the nineteenth century
            French manners and culture enjoyed a great vogue in the
            United States because of widespread support for the prin-
            ciples of the French Revolution. As early as Thomas Jef-
            ferson's first administration, the chief executive, who had
            a French chef, was criticized by Patrick Henry for "abjur-
            ing his native vituals." French cuisine made a distinct im-
            pression on American society during this period, with the
            French word "hotel" replacing "inn," "chef" ousting "cook,"
            and "restaurant" becoming popular in the American vocabu-
            lary. Omelettes, artichokes and bread made with yeast
            were among the culinary contributions of France to the
            United States. In addition, French clothing flooded the
            American market, and Jefferson, Madison, Monroe, Jackson,
            and Polk all ordered from France such items for the White
            House as furniture, silverware, and candelabras.

            Beginning about 1800 the French influence on American art
            became pronounced. Two early Republican forerunners of

this trend were John Vanderlyn and Samuel F.B. Morse,
who studied their profession in Paris.

September. A convention was signed in Paris ending the undeclared naval war between France and the United States.
Napoleon I did not insist on a renewal of the treaty of 1778
and the United States did not press for French payment of
damage claims by American shippers.

October 1. Spain ceded Louisiana to France under the terms
of the Treaty of San Ildefonso. The treaty was kept secret
for some time.

Fall. In a bitter election the Federalists berated their op-
ponents as Jacobins and accused France of a plot to sever
Kentucky from the Union. In New York City, hundreds of
French residents turned out to vote for the Republican candidate for president, Thomas Jefferson. Philip Livingston,
for one, believed that the French and Irish vote in New York
City gave the election to Jefferson. The Federalists fell,
never to rise again.

1801            Thomas Blanchard invented, at the age of thirteen, an apple-
picking machine that revolutionized the drying of fruit.

Perrin du Lac, a French traveler in the United States, found
only 160 people of the 600 families who migrated to Gallipolis, Ohio, still residing in that area.

With the election of 1800 deadlocked between Aaron Burr
and Thomas Jefferson, two men of Huguenot ancestry, James
A. Bayard and Alexander Hamilton combined their oratori-
cal skills to insure the elction of Jefferson.

Abraham Albert Gallatin was appointed secretary of the
treasury during the Jefferson administration. By the end of
the first administration Gallatin had a treasury surplus of
$1,000,000.

1802            Eleuthere Irénée du Pont de Nemours established a gunpowder works at Wilmington, Delaware, the forerunner of the
modern du Pont enterprises.

Napoleon Bonaparte became first consul and declared that
emigres could apply for repatriation and restoration of property. With this, many Royalist refugees in the United States
left for France.

Napoleon established a French educational system including communes handling primary education, state secondary schools called lycées, and municipal or private schools called colleges. This system became the model for many such state systems in the United States.

In the early part of the decade from 1800 to 1809, Louis and Hyacinth Peugnet began the "Frères Peugnet School, " the most fashionable private school in New York City. Among the pupils of the two Royalists was the future General P.G. T. Beauregard.

1803  New Orleans handled over $2,000,000 in exports and $ 2,500,000 in imports. Exports included 34,000 bales of cotton, 4,500 hogsheds of sugar, 2,000 barrels of molasses, 50,000 barrels of flour, 3,000 barrels of beef and pork, 2,000 barrels of tobacco, $500,000 worth of rice, indigo, lumber, and other crops.

January 12. In order to insure American access to the port of New Orleans, President Jefferson sent James Monroe to France with an offer of $10, 000,000 for New Orleans and West Florida.

February 4. The first American stage production of a French play occurred when Dunlap adapted the mélodrame Le Jugement de Salomon by L.C. Caigniez.

April 30. The United States purchased the entire Louisiana Territory from France for approximately $15,000,000. The purchase increased the total size of the United States by 140 percent.

October 26. In a special session of Congress called by President Jefferson, the Louisiana Purchase was ratified.

November 30. At a ceremony in the Place d'Armes, amid general rejoicing by the populace, Peter Clement Laussat assumed control of Louisiana for the French Republic. (See document, page 142).

December 20. At the Cabildo in New Orleans, Peter Clement Laussat turned over control of Louisiana to United States representatives William C.C. Claiborne and James Wilkinson. Louisiana officially became a territory of the United States.

1804      Stephen Decatur, of Huguenot ancestry, became the hero of the Tripolitan War by capturing and burning the frigate <u>Philadelphia</u>.

John James Audubon arrived in the United States at age nineteen.

1805      The Louisiana legislature created the College d'Orleans, under the presidency of Jules d'Avezac, as a representative institution for French culture.

1806      Importing houses in Philadelphia and New York reported doing a booming business in French attire, especially gloves and lace imported from Rochelle.

Thomas Blanchard invented a machine for making tacks that revolutionized the industry. He was eighteen years old.

When Zebulon Pike reached the Osage River he found that the Chouteau family had been there for twenty years, with exclusive trading privileges granted by the French and Spanish governments.

Napoleon established the University of France as a national system of secondary education. Its organization became a model for many state institutions in the United States.

Between 1806 and 1809, about 6,000 refugees landed in New Orleans after being evicted from Spanish possessions in the West Indies. About 2,000 were white, the remainder were blacks.

1808      An apparent Royalist sympathizer settled near Georgetown, New York, under the name Lewis Anathe Muller. He lived as a feudal lord for about six years, then left for France when Napoleon's downfall became imminent. His true identity remains unknown, though various researchers have identified him as Charles X, the Duc d'Angoulême, the Duc de Berry, and others. All that is really known of him was that he had been general of a division and a government official.

March. The civil code adopted in New Orleans was largely based on the Code Napoleon instituted in 1804. The bulk of the original remains in force today.

April 17. Napoleon's Bayonne Decree ordered the seizure

of all United States ships in French harbors. This amounted
to some $10,000,000 worth of ships and cargo.

1809      Joseph François Mangin designed the first St. Patrick's Ca-
thedral in New York City, 1809-1815.

Dr. Antoine François Saugrain de Vigni administered the
first smallpox vaccine in St. Louis.

Dr. François Marie Prevost performed successful Caesar-
ean operations in Louisiana.

Nicolas Appert, a French winemaker and food supplier, invented the basic process of canning food later used in the
United States.

February 25. Thomas Jefferson wrote to thank Henri Gregoire for supplying him with a copy of Literature of Negroes.
Jefferson had expressed the feeling that blacks were mentally inferior to whites, a position he retracted after reading the book that Gregoire sent to him.

1810      John Louis Ann Magdalen Lefebvre de Cheverus was named
bishop of Boston, with his diocese including all of New England. He assisted in founding the Boston Athenaeum.

The Caribbean pirates were driven out of Guadaloupe and
Martinique by the British. Under Dominique You they established a new base at Barataria Bay, Louisiana. Pierre and
Jean Lafitte, who ran a blacksmith shop, operated as the
city representatives of the smugglers in New Orleans. In
October, Jean Lafitte became an active leader at Grand
Terre on Barataria Bay. The pirates became so successful
that at one point Governor William C.C. Claiborne placed a
reward of $500 on Jean Lafitte's head. Not to be outdone,
Lafitte circulated posters offering a $1,500 reward for the
governor.

When Congress refused to renew the charter of the First
Bank of the United States, Stephen Girard bought the buildings
and began the Bank of Stephen Girard as a private venture.
He arranged the finances for the War of 1812.

March 23. Napoleon's Rambouillet Decree ordered the seizure of any United States ships entering French ports.

August 5. The French foreign minister, the Duc de Cadore, announced the repeal of the Berlin and Milan Decrees effective November 1, 1810. This was an attempt to gain favor with the United States and hopefully to sway American public opinion in favor of a war with England.

1811        Joseph Jacques Ramée, a noted French architect, lived in the United States from 1811-16. While in America his most important work was the layout and buildings of Union College, Schenectady, New York (1812-13).

1812        April 8. Louisiana became the eighteenth state in the Union.

1813        Henry Placide made his theatrical debut at the age of fourteen in New York's Anthony Street Theatre. Shorty afterward Jane Placide also began her career.

Newspapers published in Louisiana included the Courrier de la Louisiane, Gazette de la Louisiane and Amis des Lois.

Bernard Xavier Philippe de Marigny de Mandeville introduced a version of the French game "hazards" into New Orleans. Among English settlers along the Mississippi it became known as Johnny Crapaud (or Crapeau), a synonym for the Louisiana Creoles. It later became known simply as "craps."

1814        The United States government called for a loan of $5,000,000 to finance the War of 1812, but only $20,000 in subscriptions was forthcoming. Stephen Girard, of Huguenot ancestry, advanced the entire sum without so much as an inquiry into interest rates.

The British government offered pirate Jean Lafitte £30,000 and a commission in the Royal Navy if he would aid them in capturing New Orleans. Lafitte instead offered his services to the United States in exchange for only a pardon.

Mlle. Adolphe (later Mme. Blanchard) appeared as the first woman tightrope dancer in the United States.

The Compagnie de New York dissolved with a debt of over one-half million francs.

July 25. Joseph Bonaparte, traveling as M. Bouchard aboard the brig Commerce, left Royan, near Bordeaux, for the United

States. Bonaparte, the king of Naples and Spain, purchased some 26,840 acres of land in New York from James le Ray and attempted, without success, to convince Napoleon I to escape from Europe. In the United States Joseph Bonaparte went by the name Comte de Survilliers.

August 25. With the defeat of Napoleon in Europe, England was free to mount a large offensive against the United States for the first time during the War of 1812. On August 25 General Robert Ross landed 4,000 British troops near Washington, D.C. He proceeded to brush aside minor American resistance and burn down the government buildings in Washington. President James Monroe later refinished much of the White House with French furniture, including some from Charles Honore Lannuier of Paris and Pierre Antoine Bellange, also of Paris.

December 23. Colonel de la Ronde, Major Gabrielle Villeré, and Dussan la Croix brought news to General Andrew Jackson that a large British invasion force was only nine miles from New Orleans at the Villeré plantation. Jackson immediately offered battle with 2,131 men, less than half of whom had seen any action at all. The delaying action succeeded and saved New Orleans from immediate occupation by the British. Many of the defending troops were French residents of New Orleans.

1815    Louis Guillaume Valentin du Bourg was consecrated bishop of New Orleans. Later, while serving in St. Louis, he introduced teaching orders of nuns and priests.

François Charles DeLérey was born in St. Charles Parish, Louisiana. He pioneered work on yellow fever.

Commodore Stephen Decatur dictated a peace treaty to the Algerian pirates.

Significant numbers of Napoleonic soldiers settled in Pennsylvania, Texas, Alabama, and Louisiana. James le Ray Chaumont built a house at Le Rayville, ten miles east of Watertown, New York, where he entertained many notable Bonapartists exiled by the new Royalist government. He acted as a broker of land for many of the French in America, who included Joseph Bonaparte, Charles and Henri Lallemand, Comte Pierre François Réal, the Marquis Emmanuel de Grouchy, Camille Arnaud, Paul Charboneau, Lefebvre-Des-

nouettes, Regnault de Saint-Jean d'Angély, Garnier de
Saintes, Generals Murat, Rigaud, Rollard, Bertrand, Lakanal, and the brothers Peugnet (Louis, Hyacinthe and Theo-
philus).

January 1. In an artillery duel near New Orleans, French
gunners under Beluche and Dominique You outshot British
veterans from the Napoleonic Wars. After the exchange
General Jackson said: "If I were ordered to storm the gates
of hell, with Captain Dominique as my lieutenant, I would
have no misgivings of the result!"

January 8. British General Packenham placed 12,000 of his
14,500 men in line and advanced on Jackson's defensive line
about five miles from New Orleans. The defenses were held
by less than 3,200 men, including only 700 regulars under
Major Ross. Jean Lafitte provided 7,500 flints for American
muskets, and large quantities of ammunition. The pirates,
many of whom were French, manned the guns at Forts Pe-
tites Coquilles, St. John, and St. Philip, while the artillery
pieces along the American defenses were commanded by
Beluche and You. The American system of defense was engineered by Major Lacarriere Latour. A Napoleonic soldier
named Lefebvre commanded the American mortars, while
general Moreau suggested the points of defense. General
Humbert, another soldier of Napoleon, commanded the French
unit from New Orleans in the battle (See document, page 144).
while most of the American guns were actually served by
veterans of LeClerc's expedition to Santo Domingo. Gar-
rigues de Flaugeac, a state senator and brigadier general
in the Louisiana Legion also saw action in the battle. When
the results were in, American losses totalled 13 killed, 39
wounded and 19 missing. The British suffered over 3,000
casualties. New Orleans was saved, and the Baratarian pirates were pardoned by President James Monroe.

1816            Elias Boudinot, a founder of the American Bible Society, be-
                came its first president.

                Jacques Philippe Villeré became the first Creole governor
                of Louisiana, 1816-20.

                Claude Crozet, engineering instructor at West Point, 1816-
                23, began the study of descriptive geometry.

                Francis Hall grumbled that American ladies "think they import Parisian graces with Parisian bonnets." Hall, who doubted that they had any graces at all, held American women in contempt for scoffing at their own dances and preferring French "cotillions."

In Albany, New York, a French waxworks opened whose exhibits displayed "a ghastly semblance of life."

Stephen Decatur, at a dinner in Virginia, offered the following toast: "Our Country! In her intercourse with foreign governments may she always be in the right; but our country, right or wrong."

July 2. Joseph Napoleon purchased the estate of Point Breeze on the Delaware River near Bordentown, New Jersey. Through additional purchases the 211 acres were increased to 1800. A mansion was constructed that was filled with priceless works of art and visited by many French dignitaries.

1817    Thomas Hopkins Gallaudet organized the Hartford Institution for Deaf Mutes in Connecticut, the first institution for the deaf in the United States. Based on the principles of Abbé Sicard, the school employed a French teacher. Gallaudet also established teachers' training schools in Connecticut, promoted the education of blacks, advanced higher education for women, and worked for the introduction of manual training into school curricula.

Gabriel Richard was the cofounder of the University of Michigan.

March 3. The United States Congress officially granted four townships, each six miles square, along the Tombigbee River in Alabama to Napoleonic refugees at two dollars per acre.

1818    General Rigaud, Charles Lallemand and Henri Lallemand formed a colony in Texas with between 300 and 400 colonists. The colony of Champ d'Aisle on the Trinity River failed in a few years' time.

Solomon Laurent Juneau established a trading agency that grew into modern Milwaukee, Wisconsin.

Rose Philippine Duchesne founded schools of the Society of the Sacred Heart in Missouri and Louisiana.

A group of Bonapartists settled at Demopolis, Alabama, and
attempted to cultivate vines and olives. Poor surveys forced
them to move twice, but the presence of many leading Bona-
partist supporters in Alabama raised fears among Royalists
that there would be an invasion of Mexico aimed at making
Joseph Napoleon the emperor of Mexico. French personali-
ties in the colony included Lefebvre-Desnouettes, Nicholas
Raoul, Paniers, and the editors of L'Abeille Américaine,
Cluis and Simon Chaudron.

In New York, Joseph Napoleon built four homes. The main
one, half home and half fortress, was at Natural Bridge. A
second house was constructed at Alpina on the south end of
Lake Bonaparte. A hunting lodge was erected on the east
end of the lake, and a home for Annette Savage, his mistress,
went up at Evans Mills.

December. Ambrose Maréchal, a French Sulpician, became
archbishop of Baltimore. For ten years he led American
Catholics, beginning a period of ethnic conflict between
French and Irish Catholics in America.

1819    Benjamin Latrobe served as architect for the Second Bank
of the United States in Philadelphia.

Mme. Adolphe, noted French tightrope walker, debuted in
New York City.

Abbé Dominique Georges Frédéric de Riom de Prolhiac de
Fourt de Pradt formulated the two basic principles of the
Monroe Doctrine of 1823 and predicted that they would form
the basis of an American foreign policy. Thomas Jefferson
read the Abbé de Pradt and thus became a leading advocate
of the "doctrine of two spheres" principle later applied, no
doubt through his influence, by President Monroe in his his-
toric pronouncement.

During years of trading recession, only France increased
her exports to the United States. The most important products were manufactured goods and luxury items.

1820    Thomas Blanchard invented a machine for making inter-
changeable gun stocks, thus speeding the acceptance of in-
terchangeable parts in American manufacturing.

During the spring the most popular play in New Orleans was
Les Grenadiers Français.

John J. Audubon was hired by the Western Museum Society
in Cincinnati to stuff fish at $125 per month.

About 1819-20 Jacques Laramie became the first European
to visit the upper course of the Laramie River.

Gabriel Franchère published Relation d'un Voyage à la Côte
du Nord Ouest de l'Amérique Septentrionale, later used by
Senator Benton during the Oregon controversy. Washington
Irving relied on them as a source for his Astoria.

1821        Joseph Lakanal, president of the Collège d'Orleans, began
            instruction and collections in natural history.

            May 5. Napoleon Bonaparte died at St. Helena, triggering
            sorrow in New Orleans and elsewhere in the United States.

1822        June 6. William Beaumont, a U.S. Army doctor stationed
            at Ft. Mackinac, came across a French-Canadian with a
            buckshot hole in the side. Through the hole he observed the
            actions of the gastric juices and the effects of various stimu-
            lants. He published his observations in 1833 as Experiments
            and Observations on the Gastric Juice and the Physiology of
            Digestion, which became a classic of clinical medicine and
            laid the foundations for the physiology of digestion and the
            science of nutrition.

            October 20. At the Congress of Vienna, France asked the
            Quadruple Alliance to intervene in the New World to restore
            the Spanish and Portuguese empires. This led some Ameri-
            can leaders to fear European interference in the Western
            Hemisphere and led to the formulation of the Monroe Doc-
            trine.

1823        October 9. George Canning, United States minister to Bri-
            tain, secured from the French ambassador to Great Britain
            the Polignac Memorandum, an agreement that France would
            not intervene in South America. Many historians consider
            this to have been more important at the time than the Mon-
            roe Doctrine itself.

            December 2. James Monroe issued the Monroe Doctrine
            stating the principles of two hemispheres, no transfer, non-
            intervention, and nonentanglement. Much of the doctrine
            stemmed from French influence, and much of its success
            lay in the Polignac Memorandum.

1824   Antoine Imbert arrived in the United States. He later established the first lithographic firm in New York.

During the election campaign in 1824 vests were imported
from France, each adorned with a picture of Jackson, Adams,
or Clay, as the customer might wish.

Étienne Provost, a trapper, became one of the first Europeans to view the Great Salt Lake, though some dispute his
claims.

Madame Jenika de Feriet, who had purchased land along the
Black River in New York, completed her mansion called
the Hermitage. Completed at a cost of $20,000, the home
of this French Republican was finished in an ornate style
with expensive furnishings.

1825   Joel R. Poinsett was appointed as the first minister to
Mexico.

January 1. Both Houses of Congress threw a dinner for the
Marquis de Lafayette, whose visit to the United States
caused general celebrations in many American cities. In
attendance at the Congressional dinner for Lafayette, held
at the Williamson Hotel, were the president, some 30 government officials, and 150 members of Congress.

1826   Jean Dubois was consecrated bishop of New York. Of six
American bishops, the five at Baltimore, New York, Bards-
town, Boston, and Louisiana were French.

James Fenimore Cooper left for France to begin a seven-
year residence where he completed The Prairie. In Paris
he was charmed by the gaiety and brilliance of French society.

New York City Hall was designed in the distinctive style of
Louis XVI. It was one of the best early examples of French
influence in the northern United States.

1827   The first Mardi Gras was organized in New Orleans by
French-American students.

François Delaup established L'Abeille de la Nouvelle Orleans which lasted until 1923.

John James Audubon published his epic, multivolume work Birds in America between 1827 and 1838. It contained a series of 1065 crayon and watercolor pictures.

1828    February 7. Mme. Francisquy Hutin established her "modern French school of dancing" at the Bowery Theatre in New York City. The abbreviated skirts of the female performers met with hisses of moral reproach.

1830    Barthélemy Thimonnier, a French tailor, invented the sewing machine, which later had drastic effects on American industrialization.

Louis Antoine Godey began publishing Godey's Lady's Book, the first American magazine for women.

1831    André Bienvenu Roman served as an outstanding Whig governor of Louisiana, 1831-35 and 1839-43. He led early efforts at flood control, public schools, and other internal improvements.

Stephen Girard died, leaving a huge fortune to found Girard College in Philadelphia "for educating poor white orphan boys."

May. Alexander de Tocqueville arrived in the United States. He visited until February, 1832, gathering materials for his historical writings on the United States.

Autumn. Chabert entertained New York society by "entering red hot ovens, swallowing boiling oil, putting his hands in melting lead," and doing other marvels of a similar character.

1832    Between 1832 and 1835 Benjamin Louis Eulalie de Bonneville conducted a fur hunting expedition with Washington Irving as his partisan.

Antoine Robidou established Fort Robidou as a famous trapper's rendezvous in northeastern Utah.

1833    John Greenleaf Whittier, of Huguenot ancestry on his mother's side, began a thirty-year career as an Abolitionist.

1834    Edmund Ravenel published the first catalogue of marine species in the United States, listing some 735 from his private collection.

Michael B. Menard claimed the site on which he organized
a company for the development of the future city of Galves-
ton, Texas.

George Healy, an American artist, arrived in Paris to begin
what became a sixteen year stay. His most famous works
included Franklin Pleading the Cause of the American Colonies and Webster Replying to Hayne. In 1855 he received a
gold medal from the Paris Salon for the latter of these works.

Louis Philippe wrote a personal letter to Andrew Jackson in
which he made the point that "a war between the United States
and France would be especially disastrous to the wine-grow-
ing districts, and that the interests of those provinces could
be relied upon to oppose it."

June 21. On hearing of the death of the Marquis de Lafayette,
the United States House of Representatives appointed one
member from each state to a committee to honor his memory.

December 31. John Quincy Adams gave a two hour and fifty
minute oration on General Lafayette to packed galleries in
the U.S. House of Representatives.

Arthur Brisbane brought to the United States the philosophies
of Charles Fourier, as stated in Traité de l'Association Do-
mestique-Agricole.

Currier and Ives was established as a large publisher of in-
expensive lithographs.

1835    Joseph Napoleon sold his New York holdings to John La Farge
for $80,000. La Farge established modern Lafargeville,
New York, but sold the property to Bishop du Bois in 1837.
Du Bois then established a seminary, which was later moved
to New York as Fordham University.

Colonel James Bowie invented the "Bowie knife."

Alexis de Toqueville published Democracy in America, in
which he used the United States as a model for his ideal
democratic state of the future.

1836    Angelina Grimké wrote Appeal to the Christian Women of
the South, an antislavery tract that was publicly burned in

Charleston, South Carolina. Angelina and her sister Sarah were pioneer abolitionists in South Carolina, and were eventually driven north because of their beliefs.

March 6. The Alamo, defended by 200 Texas and other volunteers under Colonels William Travis, James Bowie, and Davy Crockett, fell to an army of between 3,000 and 4,000 Mexican soldiers under General Santa Anna.

1837
Many Canadian political refugees fled to the United States after the unsuccessful revolts of 1837 and 1838. These included large numbers of French-Canadians who settled in Illinois, Michigan, and Wisconsin to purchase cheap lands. Others migrated to New York and New England to become farm laborers, lumbermen, or work in brickyards or textile mills.

1838
The French-Canadian population of Burlington, Vermont, grew to the extent that Ludger Duvernay established Le Patriote, catering to the Canadian revolutionaries of 1837-39.

Mirabeau Buonaparte Lamar succeeded Sam Houston as the second president of the Republic of Texas.

Octave Chanute arrived in the United States. After building bridges and railroads, he perfected a glider by the 1890s. He invented the Chanute biplane, which served as a model for the Wright brothers.

Philippe Ricord published a classic medical book on venereal diseases, Traité pratique des maladies vénériennes.

Nicolas Marie Alexandre Vattemare, a ventriloquist and impersonator, made his American debut in New York City. Impressed by the duplication in American libraries, he put forth the idea of a library exchange system. One result of his ideas was the establishment of the Boston Public Library.

Etienne Cabet published a communistic social doctrine in Voyage en Icarie. He hoped to establish a Utopian community on the Red River in Texas, but failed.

L.J.M. Daguerre made public his daguerrotype process of photography. It became very popular in the United States, particularly during the Civil War era.

September 25. France recognized the independence of Texas from Mexico, the first European nation to do so.

1840        Richard Henry Dana, Jr.,of Huguenot ancestry, published the American classic <u>Two</u> <u>Years</u> <u>Before</u> <u>the</u> <u>Mast</u>.

Théodore Frédéric Gaillardet revitalized the <u>Courrier</u> <u>des</u> <u>États-Unis</u>, making it a national Franco-American periodical.

Bishop Du Bois purchased the La Farge mansion house for use as a Catholic theology seminary. It was later moved to New York City as St. John's College and is now Fordham University.

1841        John C. Frémont began his famous western explorations, which continued through 1845.

Father Pierre Jean de Smet established St. Mary's Mission in the Bitter Root Valley.

Hugh Legaré became United States attorney-general.

Fourierist Societies were formed in the United States under the influence of the phalanx system devised by French sociologist François Fourier. Most famous among the forty phalanxes, or farming communities, was the Brook Farm run by trancendentalists in Massachusetts from 1841 to 1860.

On a visit to the United States, the Prince de Joinville made a special effort to meet and speak to Eleazar Williams, a man raised by Indians in New York and educated in New England. Williams, who did not possess any identifiable Indian features, strongly resembled the Bourbon family of France. Many people have since claimed that Williams was indeed the escaped Dauphin, thought to have died in France.

1842        Father Edward Sorin, a French priest, founded a French seminary on land donated by another French priest,Father Stephen Badin. In 1844 the college was chartered as the University of Notre Dame. It has been said that the "final triumph of Catholic Gael over Catholic Gall was consummated when this magnificent gift of French culture came to be known known as the home of the 'Fighting Irish'."

The term "millionaire" was coined in newspapers reporting the death of tobacco magnate and banker Pierre Lorillard.

1843        Daniel Decatur Emmett organized the first minstrel troupe

to perform in New York City. As the Virginia Minstrels they
became the first minstrel group to achieve widespread popularity.

1844   Alexandre Dumas's The Three Musketeers was published
for the first time in the United States and sold over 1,000,000
copies.

Francis N. Blanchet became archbishop of Oregon.

Father Pierre Jean de Smet brought the sisters of Notre
Dame de Namur to the United States, and founded missions
among the Coeur d'Alenes, Pend d'Oreilles and Kalispels,
as well as a central mission in the Willamette Valley.

France acted as mediator between the United States and England in the dispute over Oregon.

French landscape artist Régis François Gignoux moved to
the United States. He served as the first president of the
Brooklyn Art Academy and influenced many American artists
including George Iness. He lent a new professionalism to
American landscape painting.

1845   France established a consulate in California under Louis
Gasquet.

William Chauvenet was active in the establishment of the
United States Naval Academy at Annapolis, Maryland.

Eugène Sue published the best-selling American novel The
Wandering Jew.

1846   James D.B. DeBow began publishing in New Orleans the
Commercial Review of the South and Southwest, which became a leading publication in the South.

1847   The first state institution for juvenile delinquents opened
in Massachusetts. It was based on the French "cottage"
system devised by Frédéric Auguste Demetz in 1840.

Tulane University was chartered in Louisiana as the University of Louisiana. It was later changed to Tulane University
after a large bequest by its new namesake.

Henry Wadsworth Longfellow published Evangeline, a poem
detailing the exile of the Acadians from Nova Scotia by the
British authorities.

1848     Dr. Edouard Seguin, who pioneered in the education of the feebleminded, arrived in the United States.

Charles Étienne Arthur Gayarré began publication of a four-volume English language history of Louisiana.

In a New Orleans paper there was an account of a French gentleman named Ballanger who swore on his deathbed that he brought the dauphin to the United States and placed him among Indians in New York. This lent credence to the earlier story of Eleazar Williams being the dauphin. (See 1841).

Rev. William Passevant founded a hospital in Pittsburgh, as well as others in Chicago and Milwaukee.

Between 1848 and 1853 there was in France a conscientious effort by the French government, and by speculators, to encourage people to move to California. The French public was bombarded with propaganda such as the bimonthly Le Californie that glorified new gold discoveries on the Pacific Coast of North America.

Edmund Ravenel published Echinidae, recent and fossil of South Carolina. He was one of the leading naturalists in the United States.

February 22. A new French republic was proclaimed. It met with support in the United States, especially in New Orleans and other French communities.

1849     Anne-Thérese Guerín, known as Mother Theodore, became the foundress of the Sisters of Providence of Saint Mary of the Woods in Indiana. She established the first women's academy in the state.

September 14. The first large group of about forty French arrived in San Francisco aboard La Meuse.

October 2. Patrice Dillon wrote "La Californie dan les Derniers Mois de 1849," an excellent description of San Francisco in 1849. (See document, page 145).

Hundreds of French "Forty-Niners" flocked to California between 1849 and 1853. Among some of the French companies organized in California were La Californienne, La Toison d'or, L'Aurifère, La Fortune, La Ruche d'or, La Bretonne, Compagnie Française-Américaine, Camptoir des Deux Mondes, La Moisson d'or, L'Eldorado, and Le Nouveau Monde.

1850          John Gorrie, who had conceived of the idea of artificially cooling the air in hospitals in 1839, invented the first artificial ice-making machine. In 1851 he took out the first United States patent on mechanical refrigeration.

Pierre Soulé succeeded the deceased John C. Calhoun as the leader of the States' Rights wing of the Southern Democrats.

During the decade of the 1850s Samuel M. Kier developed a distilled oil for use as an illuminant.

The French custom of wearing beards began to sweep the United States, reaching a peak between 1860 and 1890. Though the origins of the fad are somewhat obscure, there is little doubt that it began in France and spread to the United States much as French fashions did.

November. The first shipload of retired French soldiers of the Gardes Mobiles arrived in California. They kept their military organization in the mining areas and were accused of trying to seize these lands for France.

1851          Joseph Crétin was consecrated as the first bishop of St. Paul, Minnesota.

Joel R. Poinsett died. While serving as American minister to Mexico he developed the poinsettia from a Mexican flower.

Father de Smet, missionary in the Pacific Northwest, was asked by the federal government to assist in peace negotiations with the Indians. He rendered effective service and was called upon again in 1858, 1864, 1867 and 1868.

1852          Phrases such as "white work," "white sewing," and "under wardrobe" were replaced by the French term "lingerie."

Thomas Gallaudet formed St. Ann's Church in New York City specifically for deaf mutes.

Bon Marché, a pioneering Parisian department store, instituted fixed pricing. This pattern was copied by many new American stores in the 1860s.

1853          Paul Octave Hébert was elected Democratic governor of Louisiana to serve 1853-56.

William Gates Le Duc obtained the first charter for a rail-road in the Minnesota Territory.

Edmund Ravenel became the first vice-president of the Elliott Society of Natural History.

The French population in California reached approximately 30,000.

Henry William Ravenel, a leading botanist and agricultural writer, published The Fungi Caroliniani Exsiccati in five volumes between 1853 and 1860.

1854        Henry David Thoreau published Walden, a diary of his two years spent in isolation at Walden Pond, near Concord, Massachusetts. He was a leading trancendentalist.

Count Joseph Arthur de Gobineau published his Essay on the Inequality of the Races of Man, in which he argued that race determines history and races differ mentally and physically. It was used in the South to defend the slavery system after being translated into English in 1856.

Richard M. Hunt became one of the first Americans to study architecture at the École des Beaux-Arts in Paris, 1854-57. He is regarded as the most "sophisticated exponent of the French Renaissance style" in the United States, where he designed a French chateau on New York's Fifth Avenue as a home for William K. Vanderbilt.

1855        Henry Wadsworth Longfellow, Huguenot on his mother's side, published The Song of Hiawatha.

René La Roche published a classic treatise on yellow fever.

Gallaudet College was founded in Washington, D.C., as a school for the deaf.

Victor Prosper Considérant, a Fourierist, led about 1,000 French agrarians in the founding of the Utopian community named Reunion on the Trinity River, near modern Dallas, Texas. The colony lasted about one year and then dispersed throughout the state. A few followed Considérant into a communistic group along the Sabinal River.

1856        John C. Frémont was nominated as the first candidate of the

modern Republican Party for president of the United States.
He lost the election to James Buchanan, 174 electoral votes
to 114.

Daniel William Coquillet was born. He became the first to
acclimatize the Australian ladybird beetle, which saved the
California citrus industry.

William Gates Le Duc introduced the first flour made from
Minnesota spring wheat.

Matthew Fontaine Maury published The Physical Geography
of the Sea. This work made him famous as the founder of
the modern science of hydrography. He was the first to plot
the path of the Gulf Stream, originated the modern system
of deep-sea soundings, and first suggested the concept of
a transoceanic cable.

1859        Jean Charles Faget discovered a conclusive diagnosis for
            yellow fever.

            John La Mountain flew a balloon from St. Louis, Missouri,
            to Henderson, New York, the longest air flight on record
            to that date.

            Daniel Decatur Emmett of Ohio composed the song "Dixie"
            for Bryant's Minstrels. The origin of the designation "Dixie"
            for the South apparently came from the French word "Dix"
            printed on the reverse side of ten dollar bills issued by the
            Citizen's Bank of New Orleans prior to 1860. The "Dix's
            Land," or "Dixie Land," was first applied to New Orleans,
            then to Louisiana, and finally to the entire South.

            French tightrope performer Charles Blondin walked across
            Niagara Falls on a 1,100 foot cable, 160 feet above the pre-
            cipice.

1860        In 1860 nearly 25 percent of all the cotton produced in the
            South was sold to France.

            The census of 1860 showed 10,515 natives of France resid-
            ing in New Orleans. Another 5,000 lived in the rest of
            Louisiana.

            M.J. Raymond Thomassy, a French geologist, published
            Géologie pratique de la Louisiane in New Orleans and Paris.

It was the first geological survey of Louisiana. Thomassy later served on the faculties of the University of Michigan and the University of California.

Beginning in the early 1860s Édouard Manet, Claude Monet, and Paul Cézanne experimented with Impressionism, a rebellion against artistic formalism. The most gifted American Impressionist was James Whistler who loudly defended Manet in 1861.

November 8. L'Abeille, a New Orleans Creole newspaper, reflecting on the election of Lincoln, probably summed up French attitudes in Louisiana when it said: "We are for the Union so long as it is possible to preserve it. We are willing to go with Louisiana, but every good citizen is bound to use his best efforts to make Louisiana go right."

1861    Matthew Vassar endowed Vassar College as a school for women located in Poughkeepsie, New York.

January. Maj. Gustave de Coppens organized the Louisiana Zouaves, composed of Frenchmen and Italians. Their drill and dress was in the French tradition, and their commands were given in the French language. Throughout the American Civil War, zouave units, dressed in the French North African tradition of fez, baggy pants, and bright colors,were very popular in both armies. The Louisiana Tigers was another famous Southern zouave unit, while Northern counterparts included Duryea's Zouaves (5th New York) and Hawkin's Zouaves (9th New York).

April. The "Légion française" was formed as a defensive force from the French-born population of New Orleans. They adopted the uniform of the French Army, with red pants and horizon-blue jackets.

April 9. Southern artillery began the bombardment of Ft. Sumter on the orders of Brig. Gen. Pierre G.T. Beauregard. This action began the Civil War.

The Confederate government appointed J.T. Pickett as special agent to negotiate an alliance with Mexico.

The huge casualties suffered by the armies during the Civil War were largely the result of improved military technology, especially the development of the Minie ball by a French army officer .

Napoleon III, entertaining designs on Mexico, hoped to see the United States torn in two by a civil war. Soon after hostilities began he attempted to get England and Russia to intervene, but without success. The South hoped to enlist the aid of the French Army, but Napoleon III abandoned his anti-North policy after establishing Maximilian as emperor of Mexico. The Mexican government refused to receive the envoy from Richmond.

August 16. Prince Napoleon Joseph Charles Paul Bonaparte arrived in Charleston, South Carolina, as the guest of Gen. P.G.T. Beauregard.

Late in the year the Comte de Paris and the Bourbon princes arrived in the North to join the Union forces.

1862    James Leffel and Company, Springfield, Ohio, began manufacturing turbines.

François Norbert Blanchet established the first Catholic see in Portland, Oregon.

April. Brig. Gen. Benjamin Buisson, a sixty-eight year old veteran of the Napoleonic Wars, led 300 volunteers, 200 of them French, in the defense of New Orleans against Adm. David G. Farragut. Buisson had fourteen guns with which to battle Farragut's 200. Farragut, himself of French descent, captured New Orleans on May 1, thus denying its use to the Confederacy and causing Napoleon III to waver in his desire to recognize the Confederacy.

May 28. Pierre Adolph Rost resigned as minister to Spain to become a leading Confederate jurist.

September 1. Union Gen. Philip Kearney had fought in Algeria where he won the Cross of the Legion of Honor. In 1859 he served with the French Army at Magento and Solferino, receiving the decoration of the Legion of Honor from Napoleon III. He lost an arm at the siege of Mexico City, and was killed in action September 1, 1862 at the Battle of Chantilly.

September. John Slidell became a close friend of Emile Erlanger, head of the French banking house of Erlanger et Cie. Erlanger suggested a $25,000,000 loan in exchange for Confederate bonds bearing 8 percent interest. The Confederate government was, however, willing to subscribe to only $15,000,000 at 7 percent interest.

October. Napoleon III suggested to England and Russia that they cooperate in a joint note to the United States proposing a six-month armistice to consider terms for a compromise between the North and South. The other powers refused his suggestion.

December. At the Battle of Fredericksburg, Pelham's Battery, composed of Frenchmen from Mobile, Alabama, performed one of the greatest feats of artillery support in military history. While singing the Marseillaise, they delayed for an hour an assault by superior Union forces until Southern defenses were manned and ready. When Napoleon III heard of the severe Union losses at Fredericksburg he offered his good office to the United States as a peace negotiator. The offer was declined with a stiff protest against meddling in American affairs.

1863     Philip Danforth Armour entered the meatpacking business, introducing improved slaughtering techniques and usage of materials previously wasted. He purchased his own railway cars and adopted modern methods of refrigeration.

Napoleon III gave the Confederate representative John Slidell secret permission to construct ships in France. He later withdrew it in order to prevent diplomatic complications with the United States.

A. Supervièle traveled to Mexico and Paris as a representative of Confederate Gen. E. Kirby Smith.

January. Camille Armand Jules Marie, Prince de Polignac, became a brigadier general in the Confederate Army.

January 28. A contract was signed between the Confederate government and the French banking house of Erlanger et Cie. Confederate bonds selling at ninety cents on the dollar netted the South $6,250,000.

June. Napoleon III, taking advantage of American preoccupation with the Civil War, sent Archduke Maximilian to take control of Mexico. United States protests were mild, but increased as the war turned in favor of the North. (See 1866).

July 1. Union Gen. John Buford, of French descent, fired on Confederate troops, thus beginning the Battle of Gettysburg.

July 3. The Battle of Gettysburg, the turning point of the Civil War, ended with the failure of the Southern assault known as "Pickett's Charge," after Gen. George Pickett.

1864      John Greenleaf Whittier published the famous poem <u>Barbara Frietchie</u>. Whittier's mother's family name was Feuillevert, which in English means "Greenleaf."

Thomas Clark Durant organized the Crédit Mobilier.

May 30. Émile la Sene of Louisiana received Confederate credentials as commercial agent for the important post at Verz Cruz, Mexico.

August 5. Adm. David G. Farragut captured Mobile, Alabama, after uttering his famous cry, "Damn the torpedoes!"

1865      The first serious attempt to capture the spirit of French folklore was Ernest Gagnon's <u>Chansons Populaires du Canada</u>.

Robert Henri was born. Educated in France, he led the school of American realists called the "Ashcan School." Henri became the "spokesman and organizer of an assertive new independence among American artists."

The French Renaissance revival in American architecture began. Its style of mansard roofs, columns, cornices and ornamentation gave to the period from 1865 to 1885 the title "Golden Age."

1866      Croquet, a sport originating in France, was very popular in the United States.

David G. Farragut became the first full admiral in the United States Navy.

Arthur Young was born. This American cartoonist, trained in Paris by Julain and Bouguereau, awakened great sympathy for the poor through his caricatures. He has been called "the cartoonist of the masses."

Jules Guérin pioneered color printing from a half-tone block, in St. Louis, Missouri.

The Ku Klux Klan, an antiblack, anti-Catholic, anti-Jewish, anti-immigrant hate organization was founded in Tennessee.

Former Confederate Nathan Bedford Forrest was its first Grand Wizard.

Adin Ballou became a leader in the Universal Peace Union, which favored immediate disarmament, arbitration, anti-imperialism, and the abolition of military training in schools and colleges.

February 12. Secretary Seward demanded French withdrawal from Mexico. Napoleon removed his troops in the spring of 1867. Maximilian was executed by Mexican patriots on June 19, 1867.

December 27. In Chicago a gold medal was presented to Mrs. Abraham Lincoln in memory of her husband. About 40,000 Frenchmen had donated two sous apiece for the medal.

1867        Sidney Lanier published his realistic war novel Tiger Lilies.

John W. De Forest, an administrator in the Freedman's Bureau, published Miss Ravenel's Conversion from Secession to Loyalty. The novel detailed the "filthy, lecherous, half-civilized" life of poor whites in the South.

Samuel Soulé was one of three persons to whom the patent for the first typewriter was issued.

1868        Enthusiasm for cycling, a sport perfected in Paris, swept the United States.

Father de Smet, with one guide accompanying him, persuaded Sitting Bull to meet peace commissioners sent from Washington to negotiate with the Sioux.

Adam Badeau published the Military History of Ulysses S. Grant. He later aided Grant in the preparation of the general's Memoirs.

1870        By 1870 French-Canadian women formed a high percentage of female labor in New England's growing factories. French-Canadian child employees formed a higher percentage than those of any other group.

Wellesley College was chartered by Henry F. Durant.

Led by Richard M. Hunt and Henry H. Richardson, both trained at the École des Beaux-Arts in Paris, French Renaissance architecture of the Second Empire swept the United States. Furniture from the French Empire, elegant interiors, and fine ironwork exteriors had been popular since early in the nineteenth century, but were now joined by mansard roofs, cupolas and other features of the Gallic Renaissance.

From 1870 until well after World War I the École des Beaux-Arts and several private Parisian academies became a Mecca for American art students. There the young artists studied Gérôme, Cabanel, Boulanger and Carolus-Duran, as well as more contemporary French masters such as Manet, Cézanne and Monet. French-trained artists included Kenyon Cox, Abbott H. Thayer, Will Low, Carroll Beckwith, George de Forest Brush, Frank Benson, Frank Vincent du Mond, Wyatt Eaton, Francis Davis Millett, and William Morris Hunt. Some, such as Alexander Harrison, John S. Sargent, Walter Gay, Jules Stewart, William T. Dannat, and Julian Story chose to remain in France.

1871        Louis Bonard, a successful businessman, died leaving all of his property to the American Society for the Prevention of Cruelty to Animals.

The Paris Commune provoked an anti-labor union reaction in the United States. This was the first rumbling of fear in the United States of an international communist revolution. American jurists, and much of the general populace, were frightened by the threat to private property represented by the Paris Commune.

Grand Central Dépôt (later Grand Central Station) opened in New York City. Generally French in design, many critics detested its size and "monumental character."

1872        The psychological realism of Henry James took its inspiration in part from the French realists Flaubert and Balzac. James journeyed to Paris in 1872.

St. Napoleon's Church, Napoleonville, Louisiana, was consecrated by Archbishop Napoleon Joseph Perché of Angers, France. The community contained many descendants of former Bonapartists.

1874        Joseph Le Conte, professor of geology in the University of California, wrote Religion and Science on the controversy between science and theology.

His brother, John L. Le Conte, a prominent American entomologist who had been the first to map the faunal areas of the American West, became president of the American Association for the Advancement of Science.

1875    The Franco-American Union was formed. It raised money in France for the construction of the Statue of Liberty. (See 1886.)

The first organized hockey game was played between two groups of students from Montréal's McGill University. Deriving its name from <u>hoquet,</u> a French shepherd's crook, the game soon became popular throughout Canada and was brought to the United States first by French-Canadians migrating to New York and New England.

1876    At a time when mural art was largely unknown in the United States, John La Farge helped decorate Trinity Church in Boston with exquisite stained-glass windows and the most beautiful mural of the day, <u>The Ascension.</u> La Farge, called the "father of mural painting in America," also invented opaline glass for stained-glass windows, thus creating a new art and a new industry. He also did the old St. Thomas Church in New York City.

Henry H. Richardson used a French Romanesque architecture, modified somewhat for American use, in designing Boston's Trinity Church on Copley Square. The artists employed on the project included painter and muralist John La Farge and sculptor Augustus Saint-Gaudens.

Calvert Vaux assisted in the design of Central Park in New York City.

1877    American Paris-trained artists banded together to form the Society of American Artists. It existed for thirty-five years as the most distinguished exhibiting body in New York. It succeeded in liberalizing American art and gaining acceptance for young artists with new styles.

1878    Henry William Ravenel, a botanist and agricultural writer, published his eight-volume work <u>Fungi Americani Exsiccati</u> between 1878 and 1882.

Lafcadio Hearn, of Irish-Greek extraction, wrote of the New Orleans Creoles in <u>The Glamour of New Orleans.</u>

1879          Albion W. Tourgée, a Union veteran and carpetbagger in
              North Carolina, published A Fool's Errand, describing the
              brutality of the Ku Klux Klan and the failure of Southern
              jurors to grant justice to freedmen.

              George Washington Cable popularized New Orleans Creole
              culture in his novel Old Creole Days. He continued to por-
              tray Creole life in The Grandissimes (1880), The Creoles
              of Louisiana (1884), and Bonaventure (1888), the latter
              stressing the pastoral beauty of Cajun country in southern
              Louisiana.

1880          For the first time, French-Canadians won town elections
              in Manchester, New Hampshire, Lewiston, Maine, and
              Woonsocket, Rhode Island.

              John Gruelle, the American cartoonist and writer best re-
              membered for his Raggedy Ann books, was born.

              Sidney Lanier published Science of English Verse, a review
              of his years of experimentation in poetry.

              During the 1880s the master sculptor in the United States
              was Augustus Saint-Gaudens. His most famous works in-
              cluded the statue of Abraham Lincoln in Chicago's Lincoln
              Park and the Shaw Memorial. The latter, on the Boston Com-
              mon, was dedicated to Robert G. Shaw and his regiment of
              black soldiers in the Civil War.

              During the 1880s Augustin Chevalier executed the basso re-
              lievos of Union Bank in Baltimore, and designed the façade
              of the Maryland Insurance Office.

              During the period between 1880-1910 a struggle for power
              developed in New England between French and Irish immi-
              grants. A bitter feud developed between French-Canadian
              Catholics and the Irish bishops, and a political struggle en-
              sued between French-Canadian Republicans and Irish Demo-
              crats.

              Writing during the 1880s under the pseudonym Alice French,
              Octave Thanet was one of the first to discuss race relations,
              mores, and the tragic lives of poor blacks and poor whites
              in the South. She stressed the economic plight of the South
              and the degradation of sharecroppers.

Adam Badeau, U.S. Grant's military secretary, originated the term "New South" to describe the industrial movement in the southern states.

Philip Danforth Armour began the preparation of canned meats on a large scale.

At a time when Americans were rejecting German and Italian operas, Oscar Hammerstein succeeded in popularizing French plays and engaging singers trained in the Parisian school.

January 1. Ferdinande de Lesseps, daughter of engineer Ferdinand de Lesseps, broke ground for the Panama Canal.

November 8. French actress Sarah Bernhardt debuted and won critical acclaim in Dumas's La Dame aux Camélias.

1881    A monument to Huguenot settlers was erected in Oxford, Massachusetts.

Augustus Saint-Gaudens completed his statue Admiral Farragut for Madison Square Garden.

Joseph Frederic Klein began to create and develop the engineering school at Lehigh University.

July 2. Charles J. Guiteau, a disgruntled office-seeker, shot President James A. Garfield, who died September 19. Chester A. Arthur succeeded to the Presidency. Guiteau was hanged in Washington, D.C., on June 30, 1882.

1882    L'Abbé Constantin, the first pro-Catholic book published in the United States to become a best-seller, was written by French author Ludovic Halévy.

1883    The Huguenot Society of America was founded with the Honorable John Jay as its first president.

1884    Paul Tulane, a New Orleans merchant and philanthropist, donated property whose income made possible the conversion of the University of Louisiana, a state institution, into the independent Tulane University.

Dr. Edward Trudeau, a pioneer in tuberculosis research, founded the first sanitarium for tuberculosis at Saranac

Lake, New York. The first laboratory for the study of the disease was erected there in 1894.

Guy Pène du Bois was born in New York. He became the most prominent painter of New York night life, and was a pupil of Chase, Henri and Du Mond, and of Steinlen in Paris.

Professor Edouard de Laboulaye suggested the erection of a statue to commemorate the alliance between France and the United States. (See 1886).

1885      The Huguenot Society of South Carolina was founded.

Robert M. La Follette was elected to Congress, serving until 1891. During his tenure in the House he was a leading Populist. He was elected governor of Wisconsin in 1900.

Augustus Thébaud, who wrote significant studies on immigration and social problems, died.

1886      H. Jeanneret executed a famous wood engraving of the Haymarket riot in Chicago.

William Gillette's Held by the Enemy was the first important dramatic work concerning the American Civil War.

October 28. President Grover Cleveland dedicated the statue of Liberty Enlightening the World on Bedloe's Island, which was itself named after a Huguenot. The Statue of Liberty was suggested by journalist-politician Edouard René Lefebvre de Laboulay and executed by Frédéric Auguste Bartholdi. The $800,000 needed to erect the world's largest statue was raised by subscriptions in France.

1888      Joseph Le Conte published Evolution; its History, its Evidences, and its Relation to Religious Thought. It dealt with the controversy between science and theology.

Maurice Chevalier, one of the foremost celebrities of the entertainment world during the twentieth century, who made many movies and appearances in the United States, was born in Paris, France.

1889      By 1889 the factories of James B. Duke were producing half of the total American cigarette production.

Gustaf de Laval designed the first modern steam turbine.

Napoléon Le Brun designed one of the earliest successful "skyscrapers," the Metropolitan Life Building in New York City.

At the Paris Exposition John La Farge was awarded the decoration of the Legion of Honor for his exhibit of stained-glass work. His most outstanding work was probably the Battle Window at Harvard University.

February 4. The French Interoceanic Canal Company, attempting the construction of the Panama Canal, was liquidated due to monetary problems.

July 14. The centennial of "Bastille Day" brought widespread celebrations in Franco-American communities as far west as San Francisco.

1890      In 1890 the French-born population of Texas was 2,730. In addition there were 293 French-Canadians.

James Buchanan Duke formed the American Tobacco Company.

The modernist movement began in France in opposition to the impersonality of Impressionism. Precursors of the movement included Vincent van Gogh, Paul Gaugin, and Paul Cézanne. It gained widespread popularity in the United States.

During the 1890s French naturalist writer Émile Zola gave the new school of pessimistic writers the principle of scientific detachment in the portrayal of man and his experience. His influence can be seen in Frank Norris's The Pit, centered on Chicago's wheat speculators, and The Octopus, dealing with California wheat raisers fighting against exploitation by the railroads. Elements of Zola can also be seen in the nationalistic novel McTeague (1899) and in the work of Stephen Crane (see 1892).

1891      John H.B. La Trobe died. He aided Samuel F.B. Morse in installing the first telegraph and invented the La Trobe stove.

1892      Darius Milhaud, the noted composer, was born at Aix-en-Provence, France.

Pierre de Coubertin, a Parisian baron, suggested the revival of the Olympic Games.

The influence of the naturalist Émile Zola was unmistakeable in Stephen Crane's first novel, Maggie: A Girl of the Streets.

September. The first automobile in the United States was built by Charles and Frank Duryea.

1893      The façade of the Boston Public Library, begun in 1893, showed the influences of the Bibliothèque Ste. Geneviève, constructed in Paris in 1843-50. Among the artists who worked on the Boston Public Library were Augustus Saint-Gaudens and Puvis de Chavannes.

Thomas F. Bayard was appointed ambassador to Great Britain.

French architecture was used as a model for the administration building at the World Columbian Exposition. As a result of its prominence at the exposition, the art of the École des Beaux-Arts swept the country.

1894      The rich humor and folklore of the mid-Louisiana Cajuns was the topic of Bayou Folk by Kate Chopin (née Katherine O'Flaherty).

The Huguenot Historical Society was established to preserve and restore French historical materials, architecture, and so on. Today it maintains a library of over 3,000 Huguenot-related books and manuscripts at New Paltz, New York.

The American Chamber of Commerce in France was founded.

1895      Jesse C. Burkett, playing for Cleveland, led the National Baseball League in batting with a .423 average.

August 31. John Brallier was paid ten dollars and expenses to quarterback Latrobe, Pennsylvania in a football game against Jeannette, Pennsylvania. He was the first "professional" football player in the United States.

Thanksgiving Day. The Duryea brothers won the Chicago Times-Herald automobile race.

1896      Jesse C. Burkett won the baseball batting championship,
          hitting .410 for Cleveland of the National League.

          Edward Delahanty led the National League with thirteen
          home runs for Philadelphia.

          L'Association Canada-Américaine was established.

          Octave Chanute conducted the first scientific glider experi-
          ments in the United States. He designed the Chanute biplane,
          which served as a model for the Wright brothers.

          The French Chamber of Commerce of the United States was
          formed.

1897      Napoleon Lajoie led the National League with ten home runs
          (for Philadelphia).

          Rev. Edward O. Guerrant began the American Inland Mis-
          sion, aimed at providing religious aid to rural and destitute
          areas.

          Edward L. Cournand was born in Paris. He later became
          president and director of Lanvin Parfums, Inc.

          The French Bulldog Club of America was established in af-
          filiation with the American Kennel Club.

          The New York Public Library, an excellent example of the
          École de Beaux-Arts, was begun.

1898      French architecture devised the "telephone-pole" design
          for the large prison at Fresnes, near Paris. This became
          the standard design for American penal institutions in the
          following years.

          Gifford Pinchot was placed at the head of the new forestry
          bureau in the Department of Agriculture. Pinchot advised
          President Theodore Roosevelt, himself of Huguenot ancestry,
          to adopt a policy of setting aside large areas as permanent
          reservations. During the Roosevelt administration 148,000
          acres of land were withdrawn from public sale for the es-
          tablishment of national parks.

          Augustus Saint-Gaudens completed his statuette The Puritan,
          now in the Metropolitan Museum of Art in New York City.

A one-cent postage stamp was issued to commemorate "Marquette on the Mississippi" for the Trans-Mississippi Exposition.

During the Spanish-American War, Admiral George Dewey, of French descent, won a decisive victory over the Spanish fleet at Manila Bay in the Philippines.

The French press favored Spain during the Spanish-American War. France looked with disapproval on the growing power of the United States.

Edward Constant Seguin, who made pioneering studies of the nervous system, died. .

Charles Larpenteur, a fur trader, left a valuable historical source with the publication of his autobiography, Forty Years a Fur Trader on the Upper Missouri.

1899        Charles Boyer, who starred in many American motion pictures including Fanny, was born in Figeac, France.

Eva La Gallienne, foundress of the New York Civic Repertory Theater and cofoundress of the American Repertory Theater, was born.

Edward J. Delahanty led the National League with a .408 batting average for Philadelphia.

December 14. The Washington-Lafayette Silver Dollar was issued on the occasion of the one hundredth anniversary of the death of George Washington.

1900        Strong influences of Émile Zola and Balzac were evident in Theodore Dreiser's novel Sister Carrie.

By 1900 some 275,000 French-Canadians had been hired by New England industries.

Some 5,000,000 American school children contributed pennies for the erection of a statue of Lafayette in Paris. The work, executed by Paul Wayland Bartlett, was unveiled by the French government in the gardens of the Louvre.

David Belasco became a legendary figure through his successful production of French plays in the style of Sardou.

During the early 1900s French influence in the growth of
the American cinema was considerable. Lumière invented
the process of cinematography, while the names of Pathé,
Gaumont, and Melies were also prominent in this field.
French technicians developed the clever camera tricks that
were the backbone of the early Mack Sennett productions.

John J. Audubon and David G. Farragut were elected to the
Hall of Fame for Great Americans.

James Barrett led the National League with forty-six stolen
bases for Cincinnati.

1901      New York City passed the sweeping Tenement House Act
          aimed at cleaning up the slum areas. It was authored by
          Lawrence Veiller and Robert De Forest.

          Robert M. La Follette became the first Progressive gov-
          ernor when he was elected in Wisconsin. His famous "Wis-
          consin Idea" stressed opposition to city bosses, formation
          of a railroad commission, a corrupt practices act, and the
          direct primary. The latter of these first went into effect in
          Wisconsin in 1903.

          Jesse C. Burkett led the National League with a .382 batting
          average. Napoleon Lajoie led the American League with
          .405. Lajoie's thirteen home runs also led the American
          League.

1902      The Federation of French Alliances in the United States
          was established to support use of the French language,
          stimulate student exchanges with France, and award literary
          prizes.

          Clarence H. Beaumont was the National League batting
          champion, hitting .357. Edward J. Delahanty led the Ameri-
          can League with .376.

1903      France led the world in automobile production, out-producing
          the United States by 5,000 vehicles in 1903. Evidence of
          French influence in the American auto industry can be seen
          in the ready acceptance of such French terminology as
          "automobile," "garage," and "chauffeur."

          Napoleon Lajoie was the American League batting champion
          with a .355 average.

A treaty between France and the United States opened the
way for the United States to complete work on the Panama
Canal begun by France.

Augustus Saint-Gaudens completed the "greatest equestrian
monument of modern times," the statue Sherman depicting
the noted Civil War general.

1904          Edward J. De Coppet established the Flonzaley Quartet.

Napoleon Lajoie led the American League in batting with a
.381 average.

The Société des Professeurs Français en Amérique was established, including teachers of French in American colleges
and secondary schools.

The U.S. Postal Service issued a ten-cent "Louisiana Purchase" commemorative stamp.

The Louisiana Purchase Exposition in St. Louis featured
French baroque architecture with its curved lines and heavy,
ornate classicism. It marked the height of modern French
architectural influence on the United States.

American operatic soprano Lily Pons was born.

1905          John Merven Carrère served as architect for the U.S. Senate (1905) and the House (1906) Office Buildings.

Robert M. La Follette was elected to the first of three
terms in the United States Senate. He voted against United
States entry into World War I, opposed joining the League
of Nations, and opposed the World Court.

Alfred Binet and Théodore Simon, French psychologists,
devised a metric intelligence scale based on measuring
"mental age" in relation to "chronological age." (See 1908.)

The Juilliard Musical Foundation was established in New
York City.

John Greenleaf Whittier was elected to the Hall of Fame for
Great Americans.

Jean-Paul Sartre, the philosopher, was born in Granville,
France.

Claudette Colbert, the American actress, was born in Paris, France.

Cliff Arquette, who entertained millions with his portrayal of rustic "Charlie Weaver," was born.

Jules Verne died. He provided literary masterpieces that were very popular in the United States, including Around the World in Eighty Days and Twenty Thousand Leagues Under the Sea.

1906      Gaston Lachaise, a noted Parisian sculptor, migrated to the United States.

Alexis Carrel joined the research staff at the Rockefeller Institute for Medical Research. He was the first to sew blood vessels together, the first to keep body tissues alive in jars, and the first to transplant animal organs.

Dr. Lee De Forest invented the audion tube making amplification, and the radio, possible.

Henry Algernon du Pont was elected as an influential United States Senator from Delaware, 1906-17.

John Merven Carrère served as the architect for the New Theatre in New York City.

1907      The Alliance Française de New York was formed of persons interested in French language and culture.

David du Bois Gaillard, author of Wave Action in Relation to Engineering Structures (1904), was appointed chief of dredging and excavation on the Panama Canal by General Goethals. Harry H. Rousseau engineered the terminals designed for the canal.

1908      Gifford Pinchot was appointed chairman of the newly created National Conservation Commission.

French-Canadian immigrants elected their first governor in New England, Aram J. Pothier of Rhode Island.

The Binet-Simon intelligence tests were translated into English. Revised at Stanford University, the Stanford-Binet tests became the standard American measure of "I.Q."

The New York art world was shocked by a show of Rodin watercolors and by the first American exhibition of Matisse.

Led by Robert Henri, the "Ash Can" School revolted against the conservative National Academy of Design. They staged their own art show in New York. One of Henri's famous works was Boy With a Piccolo.

Alphonse Desjardins established the first credit union association in Massachusetts and New Hampshire. Known as La Caisse Populaire Ste. Marie, it was officially chartered in 1909. About 99 percent of the depositors were French.

Imported Parisian skirts with "fish-net" stockings became a fad in the United States. Some people were arrested for wearing this revealing attire.

1909        Toulouse-Lautrec opened his first American exhibition.

July 30. Benjamin Delahauf Foulois flew with Orville Wright on the first intercity American flight, from Ft. Myer, Virginia, to Alexandria, Virginia.

1910        Rousseau opened his first American art exhibition.

Ray Harroun was the first United States Auto Club national champion.

Pathé Frères of Paris circulated the first newsreel in the United States, a weekly edition of their Pathé Journal.

January 7. President Taft removed Gifford Pinchot from office after Pinchot opposed the sale of water-power rights, and later the sale of coal lands to private interests.

1911        John M. Carrère served as the architect for the New York Public Library.

Strong influences of Émile Zola and Balzac can be seen in Theodore Dreiser's novel Jennie Gerhardt, as well as The Financier (1912), and The Titan (1914).

The French Institute in the United States was established to disseminate French culture in the United States.

Ray Harroun won the Indianapolis "500" with a speed of 74.59 miles per hour.

January 21. The National Progressive Republican League was founded by Robert M. La Follette and others. Its platform called for the direct election of United States Senators and delegates to national conventions, initiative, referendum, recall and other progressive legislation.

1912          Alexis Carrel, an American surgeon and biologist, won the Nobel Prize for medicine. He was the author of Man, the Unknown.

Edna St. Vincent Millay wrote "Renascence."

Gaston Lachaise began work on his bronze statue Standing Woman.

The French-made film Queen Elizabeth, starring Sarah Bernhardt, opened in the United States and made motion pictures a genuine art form.

1913          The first American art exhibition of Picabia opened.

French Cubism, popularized by Picasso, Braque, and Cézanne, was introduced to America at an exhibition held in the 69th Regiment Armory in New York. Marcel Duchamp's Nude Descending a Staircase caused an avalanche of criticism and wrath from conventional critics.

The Société des Architectes Diplomes par le Gouvernement Français, Groupe Américain, was formed to encourage the study of architecture.

School children in Pierre, South Dakota, unearthed one of the many lead plates left by French explorers two centuries before.

Jules Goux won the Indianapolis "500" in a Peugeot. He averaged 75.93 miles per hour.

Francis Ouimet became the first amateur to win the U.S. Open title in golf.

Jacob E. Daubert led the National League in batting with an average of .350.

1914          Braque's first American art exhibition opened.

Ezra Pound, deeply impressed by the verse technique of

Provençal poetry, published <u>Des Imagistes</u>, an anthology of imagist verse.

Several hundred Americans volunteered for service in the French military during World War I. Many joined the French Foreign Legion, while others joined the new air forces. One of the latter, Raoul Gervais Lufbery, joined the Lafayette Escadrille and was officially credited with destroying seventeen German machines.

Jacob E. Daubert won the 1914 National league batting title with a .329 average.

1915       Edward L. Trudeau died. He was an American physician noted for his work on tuberculosis.

Pierre "Poppa" Laffitte opened his famous Restaurant Laffitte in New York City, with a specialty in French cuisine.

March 4. The La Follette Seaman's Act improved conditions for sailors in the American merchant marine.

1916       Cleveland Abbe died. This astronomer was instrumental in the establishment of the U.S. Weather Bureau.

Kenyon Cox's <u>Tradition</u> became an excellent example of the influence on American art of the École des Beaux-Arts.

April 18. A small group of American aviators reported to Captain Georges Thénault at Luxeuil, France, to form Escadrille No. 124. Known as the American Escadrille, it has come down through history as the Lafayette Escadrille.

1917       The National Hockey League was formed. Hockey apparently originated among French-Canadians and included many famous French-Canadian players throughout the next decades.

April 4-6. Robert M. La Follette made a four-hour speech as leader of the antiwar faction in the U.S. Senate. The final vote in the Senate was 82-6 in favor of war. In the House it was 313-50 in favor of war.

France sent many battle-experienced soldiers to instruct and train American troops preparing for service in World War I.

July 4. General Pershing, head of the American troops in

Europe, visited the tomb of Lafayette in Paris and noted:
"Lafayette, we are here!"

July 18. By mid-July there were a million American troops
in France.

Movie actress Danielle Darrieux was born in Bordeaux,
France.

1918        Liberal Oswald Garrison Villard, grandson of William Lloyd
Garrison, became editor of The Nation. He began a reversal
in social policy toward the dissenting tradition of his grandfather during his years as editor, 1918-33.

American troops participated in hard fighting along the
Western Front in France.

1919        The Federation of French War Veterans was established
for French veterans of World War I and later World War II.

F. Scott Fitzgerald and Ernest Hemingway went to Paris to
study.

Louis Goddu, inventor of a shoe-manufacturing machine
used throughout American industry, died.

1920        During the period of prosperity from 1920 to 1929, there
was a resurgence in French-Canadian immigration to mill
towns in New England.

American architects during the 1920s favored designing
homes along the lines of the French manoirs.

Chanel first became famous in the United States as a de-
signer of women's fashions in hats and dresses.

Sculptor Augustus Saint-Gaudens was elected to the Hall of
Fame for Great Americans.

Gaston Chevrolet won the Indianapolis "500" at a speed of
88.62 miles per hour.

1921        The heavyweight championship fight between Jack Dempsey
and Georges Carpentier of France, won by the former, was
the first fight to net gate receipts in excess of $1,000,000.
The "Fight of the Century" was broadcast by station KDKA
in Pittsburgh.

Edna St. Vincent Millay published "Second April."

1922    Nanette Fabray (Fabarés), the movie actress of French ancestry, was born in California.

The American Society of the French Legion of Honor was
established to promote French culture, strengthen Franco-
American friendship and provide a social fraternity for
members of the French Order of the Legion of Honor in the
United States.

1923    Dr. Lee De Forest invented "phonofilm," a method for placing sound on motion picture film.

Emile Coué established a clinic for the mentally ill in New
York.

Robert Henri published The Art Spirit, a compilation from
his essays and classroom notes.

Marcel Marceau, the noted pantomime actor, was born in
Strasbourg, France.

William H. Gillette, American playwright and actor, died.
He was perhaps best noted for his thirty-year characteriza-
tion of Sherlock Holmes.

Edna St. Vincent Millay won the Pulitzer Prize for The Harp
Weaver and Other Poems.

1924    An immigration act passed by Congress limited the annual
number of French immigrants into the United States to
3,000.

L. L. Corum and Joe Boyer won the Indianapolis "500" with
a speed of 98.23 miles per hour.

Jacques F. Fournier led the National League with twenty-
seven home runs.

James B. Duke established the Duke Endowment to assist
institutions such as colleges, hospitals, and orphanages in
North and South Carolina. Duke University was officially
chartered.

Robert M. La Follette conducted an unsuccessful campaign
for president on the Progressive ticket.

Claudette Colbert made her American debut, beginning a meteoric rise to stardom. Born in Paris, her real name was Lily Chauchoin.

A series of Huguenot-Walloon Tercentenary stamps was issued depicting the ship New Netherland on the one-cent denomination, the landing at New York on the two-cent issue, and the Ribaut Memorial at Mayport, Florida, on the five-cent stamp.

The Huguenot-Walloon Tercentenary half-dollar was minted to commemorate the arrival of the French and Belgian Protestants at New Amsterdam in 1624. The coin depicts Admiral Gaspard de Coligny and William the Silent, king of Holland, on the obverse, while the reverse bears the likeness of the ship New Netherland.

1925    Denise Darcel, a motion picture star, and Pierre Boulez, the conductor, were born in France.

The Paris Exposition greatly influenced American architecture toward the "modernistic" approach.

The Mutual Society of French Colonials was established as a fraternal society for French nationals and people of French parentage.

William M. Beauchamp, a noted authority on the history of the Iroquois Indians, died.

Marius Barbeau and Edward Sapir published Folk Songs of French Canada containing forty-one folksongs.

1927    French tennis star Suzanne Lenglen did much to popularize that sport in the United States.

Vernon L. Parrington, a social-democratic historian strongly influenced by French theories of equality, published his three-volume work Main Currents in American Thought.

The American Association of Teachers of French was formed from teachers at the college and secondary school levels.

The Committee of French Speaking Societies was established. It annually organized celebrations of Bastille Day and Armistice Day.

1928        Stephen Vincent Binét published "John Brown's Body."

The American Center for Students and Artists was formed
in Paris as a social and cultural center for young people
from all nations. It maintains an 8,000-volume library of
French classics, history, art, and literature.

January 17. On the tenth anniversary of American entry into
World War I, French Minister of Foreign Affairs Aristide
Briand proposed that the two governments sign a pact out-
lawing war and agreeing to settle disputes peacefully. Signed
by Secretary of State Kellogg and President Calvin Coolidge
on January 17, 1928, the Kellogg-Briand Pact eventually included the signatures of sixty-two nations.

July 4. Jean Lussier became the first man to go over Niagara Falls in a rubber ball.

1929        Stephen Vincent Binét won a Pulitzer Prize for his epic poem
"John Brown's Body."

Oliver La Farge won a Pulitzer Prize for his first novel,
Laughing Boy.

John C. Garand invented a semi-automatic rifle that was
used as the standard U.S. Army and U.S. Marine Corps
weapon during World War II.

Marius Barbeau, Paul England, and William Healey published
Chansons Canadienne, two volumes containing twenty-four
songs.

Robert G. Le Tourneau became president of Le Tourneau
Company, the world's largest manufacturer of earth-mov-
ing equipment.

1930        The census showed 21,000 French-born people residing in
New York City. Some 10,185 French resided in Texas.

During the 1930s E.H. Gauvreau edited the popular New
York Graphic.

Mary Agnes Starr began a program of French-Canadian folksongs on WHA in Wisconsin. Her recordings of voyageur
songs are now in the Library of Congress.

Roger Filiatrault, André Trottier, Émile Lamarre, and Jules

Jacob formed the folksong group Le Quatuor Alouette in Montréal.

1931      Henry Sigerist, a historian of medicine, came to the United States as a lecturer at Johns Hopkins University.

A United States commemorative stamp celebrated the 150th anniversary of the Battle of Yorktown. The stamp pictured Washington flanked by the Comte de Rochambeau and the Comte de Grasse.

Camille L. Nickerson, known as the "Louisiana Lady," began collecting and researching Creole music in New Orleans' Vieux Carré, and later in rural areas around Lafayette and St. Martinsville. She did much to popularize the ballads of those areas.

Actress Leslie Caron was born in Paris.

1933      Actor Jean-Paul Belmondo was born at Neiully-sur-Seine, France.

1934      The fashion industry in the United States launched a drive for Parisian support. In Paris, American fashion advertisers conducted a tea for forty top French fashion experts including Lelong, Callot, Patou and Chanel. The French government agreed to aid those advertising French fashions in the United States.

Claudette Colbert won an Academy Award as best actress for her performance in It Happened One Night.

The first quintuplets to live were born to Elzire and Oliva Dionne, Ontario, Canada.

1935      Brigitte Bardot, the motion picture sex-symbol, was born in Paris, France.

Will Durant began publishing his multi-volume work, The Story of Civilization.

1936      Pierre Monteux, successful conductor of the Metropolitan Opera Company, 1917-19, and the Boston Symphony Orchestra, 1919-24, became conductor of the San Francisco Symphony. He held the position until 1952, making the symphony into one of the nation's finest orchestras.

The Association Medicale Franco-Américaine was established.

Stamp collectors founded the France and Colonies Philatelic Society.

Carl Hubbell pitched twenty-four consecutive victories for the National League New York Giants, including the last sixteen decisions of 1936 and his first eight in 1937.

1937    Father John La Farge, son of the famous painter by that name, published The Race Question and the Negro. It was an early Catholic denunciation of segregation and the denial of equal economic and social opportunities.

Novelist John P. Marquand won the Pulitzer Prize for The Late George Apley.

Napoleon Lajoie was elected to the Baseball Hall of Fame. In 2,475 lifetime games between 1896 and 1916, he hit .339. He was one of less than a dozen players to accumulate 3,242 hits.

1938    Amedée Ozenfant arrived in the United States. He taught art and established a school for the fine arts in New York City.

Raymond Loewy received the American Design medal, given for industrial designing.

1939    Movie star France Nuyen was born in Marseilles, France.

René Dubois, a microbiologist and environmentalist, discovered the first commercially produced antibiotic.

Yves Tanguy, a leading surrealist, arrived in the United States. He became a naturalized citizen in 1948.

The Committee of French American Wives was established "to extend relief to French people in need, regardless of politics."

John La Touche, a lyricist, composed the words for the music of Earl Robinson. The result was a very popular leftist pseudo-folk ballad by black singer Paul Robeson, which was even performed at the 1940 Republican National Convention.

Irène Thérèse Whitfield published <u>Louisiana</u> <u>French</u> <u>Folk</u> <u>Songs</u> with phonetic Creole transcriptions.

1940        The U.S. Post Office issued a one-cent John James Audubon commemorative stamp.

With the outbreak of World War II, and the fall of France, the United States became a haven for prominent French refugees. The exiles included statesmen like Camille Chautemps, educator Philippe Le Corbeiller, theoretical physicist Léon Brillouin, mathematician Jacques Hadamand, artist Fernand Léger, and dada and surrealist writer André Breton.
        Literary figure André Maurois published <u>The</u> <u>Tragedy</u> <u>of</u> <u>France</u>, and Jules Romain penned <u>The</u> <u>Seven</u> <u>Mysteries</u> <u>of</u> <u>Europe</u>. Alexis Láger (pseud. St. John Perse) published <u>Exil</u> (1944), <u>Vents</u>, (1946), <u>Amers</u> (1957), and <u>Oiseau</u> (1962). He won the Nobel Prize for literature in 1960.
        In the field of art, dadaist Marcel Duchamp settled in New York and surrealist Yves Tanguy resided in Connecticut. Surrealists André Masson and Max Ernst journeyed to the United States, as did Ferdinand Léger, a founder of cubism. Composer Nadia Boulanger taught at the Longy School of Music in Cambridge, Massachusetts, and Darius Milhaud, who taught at Mills College, composed 182 musical pieces in the United States between 1940 and 1962. Milhaud's works include "La Libération des Antilles, " "Carnival à la Nouvelle-Orléans, "and "Un Français à New York."

June 22. France signed an armistice with Germany. The United States recognized the Vichy French government. Many people regarded this as appeasement, but it later made possible an easy invasion of North Africa in 1942.

1941        Pierre Auger, discoverer of the Auger effect, arrived in the United States.

Brig. Gen. James P.S. Devereux surrendered Wake Island to the Japanese after a brief but effective defense.

Marc Chagall, the Russian-born French artist, arrived in New York where he did some of his best works.

Lilly Daché won an award for her design of a hat for Lord and Taylor.

1942        William Rose Benet won a Pulitzer Prize for his novel in verse <u>The</u> <u>Dust</u> <u>Which</u> <u>is</u> <u>God</u>.

René Clair, a war refugee, directed the motion picture I Married a Witch.

Claire L. Chennault, organizer of the Flying Tigers, kept the Burma Road open to Allied vehicles.

1943  Jacques Cousteau, marine explorer, aided in the invention of the aqualung.

1944  Thousands of French-Americans served in the armed forces, many earning distinctions in combat areas. These included Lt. Gen. Leonard T. Gerow who won the Distinguished Service Medal, Legion of Honor, and Croix de Guerre for his leadership of the U.S. 5th Army Corps in Europe.

Louis Boudreau led the American League with a batting average of .327.

Georges Barrère died. This French-born flutist founded the Little Symphony, a wind-instrument group.

October 23. The United States recognized the French government-in-exile under Charles de Gaulle and Henri Giraud as the provisional government of France.

1945  Mathematician Jacques Hadamand published Essay on Psychology of Invention in the Mathematical Field.

The Association of the Free French in the United States was established.

Sidney Lanier was elected to the Hall of Fame for Great Americans.

Arthur Laurents published Home of the Brave.

Edward J. Delahanty was elected to the Baseball Hall of Fame.

March 18. Maurice "Rocket" Richard of the Montréal Canadiens became the first hockey player in the National Hockey League to score fifty goals in a single season.

1946  Dr. John H. Dessauer was responsible for the adoption and financing by the Haloid Company of Rochester, New York, of a new process of electrophotographic reproduction called xerography, or more popularly, xerox.

1947        Between 1947 and 1949 Gen. Lucius DuBignon Clay was com-
            mander of the "Berlin Airlift."

            French fashion designer Christian Dior created a "new look"
            in women's fashions, featuring long hemlines and full skirts.

            Maurice Richard was named the Most Valuable Player in
            the National Hockey League.

1948        Marcel Cerdan was the world middleweight boxing champion,
            1948-49.

1949        Léon Brillouin became director of research for the Watson
            Laboratory of I.B.M.

            Simone de Beauvoir published The Second Sex, which be-
            came the bible of the women's liberation movement.

            William F. Giauque won the Nobel Prize for chemistry in
            the field of chemical thermodynamics.

            René d'Harnoncourt became the director of the New York
            Museum of Modern Art.

            Pauline Trigere received the American Fashion Critics'
            Award for design in 1949 and 1951.

1950        Eddie Le Baron, the original "belly series" quarterback,
            led the college All-Stars to an upset victory over the Phila-
            delphia Eagles.

1951        J.D. Salinger published the popular novel The Catcher in
            the Rye.

            A three-cent commemorative stamp marked the 250th anni-
            versary of the landing of Antoine de la Mothe Cadillac at
            Detroit.

            The National Huguenot Society was established for Protes-
            tants who are lineal descendants of the Huguenots.

1952        The McCarran-Walter Act allowed an annual quota of 3,069
            French immigrants.

            A three-cent commemorative stamp celebrated the 175th
            anniversary of Lafayette's arrival in the United States.

Arthur Laurents published The Time of the Cuckoo.

1954        Jack Choquette won the National Modified Stock Car title with 5,402 points.

March 20. France asked the United States for a military intervention in the Vietnamese War.

April 3. Secretary of State Dulles asked a group of Congressmen to support the use of American air forces in Vietnam. The request was refused.

July 21. As a result of the inability of France to hold Vietnam, the Declaration of the Geneva Conference was formulated dividing Vietnam into two sections at the 17th Parallel.

1955        Vincent du Vigneaud of Cornell Medical College won a Nobel Prize for developing two hormones that aided in childbirth.

The Society for French Historical Studies was formed at Ohio State University in Columbus, Ohio.

The Society for French American Cultural Services and Educational Aid was established to provide materials on French history and culture.

1956        Dr. André F. Cournand won a share of the Nobel Prize for medicine by perfecting the technique of "cardiac catheterization" at Columbia University.

Jean Beliveau won the Hart Trophy as the Most Valuable Player in the National Hockey League.

Marguerite and Raoul d'Harcourt published Chansons Folkloriques Français au Canada.

November 2. France and Britain invaded Egypt. The United States favored a peaceful settlement, thus straining French-American relations.

1957        Maurice Chevalier starred in the hit movie Love in the Afternoon.

The 200th anniversary of Lafayette's birth was celebrated with a three-cent commemorative stamp.

Jacques Cousteau won an Oscar for the best documentary film feature, The Silent World. He then began his famous series of underwater explorations aboard the Calypso.

Arthur Laurents published A Clearing in the Woods.

1958    Maurice Chevalier starred in Gigi, the same movie that marked the peak of popularity for Louis Jourdan.

A twenty-five cent Paul Revere stamp was issued depicting the revolutionary hero at the age of seventy-eight.

The 200th anniversary of the fall of Ft. Duquesne to British forces was marked with the issue of a four-cent commemorative stamp.

Violette Verdy joined the New York City Ballet as a principal dancer.

1959    Simone Signoret won an Academy Award for the best acttress for her performance in Room at the Top.

Pauline Trigere was named to a Hall of Fame for Fashion Design.

1960    Maurice Chevalier, Leslie Caron, and Louis Jourdan starred in Can Can.

During the decade of the 1960s Maurice Jarée kept American audiences entertained with his Academy-Award-winning musical scores. Among his compositions were the musical themes of Lawrence of Arabia, Dr. Zhivago, Grand Prix, Is Paris Burning, and The Longest Day.

Robert Goulet debuted on Broadway in Camelot. A star of many television programs and movies, he later received a Tony Award as the best musical actor for The Happy Time, and an Emmy Award for the television version of Brigadoon.

Henry David Thoreau was elected to the Hall of Fame for Great Americans.

The victory of the Kennedy campaign for the presidency brought at least two French-Americans into prominence, Presidential Press Secretary Pierre Salinger and the First Lady, the former Jacqueline Bouvier.

1961        July 1. President Kennedy met with Charles de Gaulle at
            Versailles in an attempt to solve European economic prob-
            lems and cement relations between the United States and
            France.

1962        Goalie Jacques Plante won the Hart Trophy as the most valu-
            able player in the National Hockey League. The Calder Tro-
            phy for the best rookie went to Bobby Rousseau.

            The Salon Litteraire, Artistique et Diplomatique, was estab-
            lished in New York to promote Franco-American cultural
            ties.

1963        Louis Jourdan starred in The VIP's.

            A five-cent Audubon commemorative stamp was issued fea-
            turing the Columbia Jay, which is now in the National Gallery
            of Art, Washington, D.C.

            The Society of French-American Affairs was founded in New
            York to encourage those interested in French-American po-
            litical relations.

            August 5.  French-American relations became strained
            when France refused to sign the Nuclear Test Ban Treaty
            initiated by the United States, the U.S.S.R., and Britain.
            Its purpose was to ban nuclear testing in the atmosphere.

            Beginning in 1963 French President de Gaulle adopted an in-
            dependent, anti-American policy in which he vetoed admis-
            sion of the United Kingdom into the European Common Mar-
            ket, opposed American plans for a NATO nuclear force, re-
            fused to sign the Nuclear Test Ban Treaty, gave diplomatic
            recognition to Communist China, opposed American partici-
            pation in the Vietnam War, and insisted that NATO withdraw
            all its bases from France by 1967.

1964        A conference was held in St. Louis, dealing with the French
            in the Mississippi Valley, on the occasion of the bicentennial
            of the founding of that city.

            Jean Beliveau was awarded the Hart Trophy as the most valu-
            able player in the National Hockey League, while Jacques
            Laperriere was named Rookie of the Year.

1965        Jockey Ron Turcotte won the Preakness aboard the horse
            Tom Rolfe.

Cherilyn La Piere rose to fame with five records on the best-seller list. Teaming with Sonny Bono as Sonny and Cher, their hit record "I Got You Babe" sold over 3,000,000 copies.

During the years between 1945 and 1965 the United States sent 4.2 billion dollars' worth of economic aid to France.

October 17. A nine-foot bronze statue of Daniel Greysolon, Sieur du Luth, by Jacques Lipchitz, was unveiled on the Duluth campus of the University of Minnesota.

1966        June 6. NATO officially moved its headquarters from France to Belgium.

July 1. France officially removed its troops from NATO.

1967        March 31. NATO removed all of its troops from France.

1968        Ballerina Violette Verdy received the Capezio Award for her many contributions to dance.

Curtis Le May, the former head of the Stategic Air Command and Air Force Chief of Staff under the Kennedy administration, ran for vice-president on an independent ticket with George Wallace.

1969        René Dubos won the Pulitzer Prize for general nonfiction for So Human an Animal: How We Are Shaped by Surroundings and Events.

1970        Louis Boudreau was elected to the Baseball Hall of Fame.

October 5. James R. Cross, the senior British trade commissioner in Montréal, was kidnapped by the Front de libération du Québec.

October 10. Pierre Laporte, minister of Labor and Immigration, was kidnapped by the Front de libération du Québec.

October 17. Pierre Laport was murdered by the Front de liberation du Quebec.

1971        Cherilyn La Piere debuted in the popular "Sonny and Cher" television show.

When a federal injunction prohibited the <u>New York Times</u>
from publishing the "Pentagon Papers, " Senator Mike Gra-
vel of Alaska read portions of the documents into the record
of a Senate subcommittee.

1972            Ron Turcotte rode Riva Ridge to victory in the Kentucky
                Derby and the Belmont Stakes.

                Simone de Beauvoir published <u>The Coming of Age</u>, an ex-
                posé of Western neglect of the elderly.

1973            Ron Turcotte rode Secretariat to the Triple Crown in the
                Kentucky Derby, the Preakness, and the Belmot Stakes.

1974            Philippe Petit thrilled spectators by walking on a tightrope
                between the World Trade Towers in New York City.

                President Ford met French President Giscard d'Estaing on
                Martinique to attempt to solve energy problems and improve
                Franco-American relations.

## CARTIER ON THE BAY OF GASPÉ
### 1534

In 1534 Jacques Cartier explored the coast of
Newfoundland, entered the Strait of Belle Isle,
and sailed the Bay of Gaspé. On July 24, about
two weeks before leaving for France, Cartier
erected a cross to mark his presence at the
entrance of the Bay of Gaspé. Inscribed on it
were the words "Vive le roy de France."
Cartier's description of the event is repro-
duced below.

Source: Ralph Henry Gabriel, The Pageant of
America. New Haven: Yale University Press,
1925. From Volume 1, "Adventures in the Wilderness" by Wissler, et al, copyright United
States Publishers Association, Inc.

On Friday the 24th of July, 1534, we had a cross made, thirty feet high,
which was put together in the presence of a number of Indians on the point
at the entrance to this harbor. Under the cross-bar we fixed a shield with
three fleur-de-lis in relief, and above this a wooden inscription, engraved
in large Gothic characters: Long Live the King of France! When the cross
had been raised we all knelt down, with our hands joined, worshipping it
before the Indians. We then made signs to them, looking up to Heaven, to
show them that it was by means of the Cross that we had gained our redemp-
tion. The Indians displayed many signs of admiration, constantly turning
and gazing at the Cross.

## THE ORDER OF GOOD CHEER
### 1609

The early French explorers in the New World
found life very tenuous, especially during the
long winters that they had to endure in Canada.
A bright spot in their drab lifestyle was the
"Order of Good Cheer, " formed to provide a
varied menu and a cooperative social function,
as reported here by Marc Lescarbot in 1609.

Source: Ralph Henry Gabriel, The Pageant of
America. New Haven: Yale University Press,
1925. From Volume 1, "Adventures in the Wilderness" by Wissler et al, copyright United
States Publishers Association, Inc.

Each man was appointed chief steward in his turn. No one, two days
before his turn, failed to hunt and fish for delicious fare. The chief steward, whom the Indians called Atoctegic, marched in at evening dinner, nap-
kin on shoulder, wand of office in his hand, around his neck the Order's
collar; then, after him, every single member of the Order of Good Cheer,
each with his appropriate dish. At night, before giving God due thanks,
the steward handed the collar to his successor, each then drinking to the
other. We had abundance of game, such as duck, bustard, partridges, and
geese; also moose, caribou, bear, and rabbits, whereof we made dishes
better than those of the famous Rue aux Ours in Paris; for of all meats what
can be tenderer than the best moose, or more toothsome than good beaver
tail?

## A HUGUENOT PETITION TO THE BRITISH AMBASSADOR
### 1621

> Foreign citizens wishing to settle en masse in
> the English-speaking colonies customarily pe-
> titioned the English monarch for permission
> and often for lands upon which to settle.  The
> following petition, addressed to Sir Dudley
> Carleton, British ambassador to the Hague,
> was presented by French and Belgian Protes-
> tants, led by Jesse de Forest, in July, 1621.
>
> Source:  Lucian J. Fosdick, The French Blood
> in America.  New York:  Baker and Taylor Co.,
> 1911.

His lordship the ambassador of the most serene king of Great Britain
is humbly entreated to advise and answer us in regard to the articles which
follow.

I.  Whether it would please his Majesty to permit fifty to sixty families,
as well Walloons as French, all of the Reformed religion, to go and settle
in Virginia, a country under his rule, and whether it would please him to
undertake their protection and defense from and against all, and to maintain them in their religion.

II.  And whereas the said families might find themselves near upon
three hundred persons; and whereas they would wish to carry with them a
quantity of cattle, as well for the cultivation of the earth as for their sustenance, and for these reasons would need more than one ship; whether his
Majesty would not accommodate them with one, well equipped and furnished
with cannon and other arms, on board of which, together with the one they
would provide, they could accomplish their voyage; the same returning to
obtain merchandise for the regions granted by his said Majesty, as well as
that of the country.

III.  Whether he would permit them, on their arrival in said country,
to choose a convenient spot for their abode among the places not yet culti-
vated by those whom it has pleased his Majesty to send thither already.

IV.  Whether, having secured the said spot, they might build a city for
their protection and furnish it with the necessary fortifications, wherein
they might elect a governor and magistrates for the maintenance of order
as well as justice, under those fundamental laws which it has pleased his
Majesty to establish in said regions.

V.  Whether his said Majesty would furnish them cannons and munitions
for the defense of said place, and grant them right in case of necessity to
make powder, fabricate balls and found cannons under the flag and arms
of his said Majesty.

VI.   Whether he would grant them a circuit or territory of eight English miles radius, that is sixteen in diameter, wherein they might cultivate fields, meadows, vineyards, and the like, which territory they would hold, whether conjointly or severally, from his Majesty in such fealty and homage as his Majesty should find reasonable, without allowing any other to dwell there unless by taking out papers of residence within said territory, wherein they would reserve rights of inferior lordship; and whether those of them who could live as nobles would be permitted to style themselves such.

VII.   Whether they would be permitted in the said lands to hunt all game, whether furred or feathered, to fish in the sea and rivers, and to cut heavy and small timber, as well as for navigation as other purposes, according to desire; in a word, whether they might make use of everything above and below ground according to their will and pleasure, saving the royal rights; and trade in everything with such persons as should be thereto privileged.

## RELIGIOUS PERSECUTION IN LA ROCHELLE
### 1685

Many French Protestants migrated to the United
States due to the persecutions carried on against
their religious group in France. The following
letter, dated October 1, 1685, was sent to an
American from La Rochelle, a strong center of
French Protestantism.

Source: Lucian J. Fosdick, The French Blood
in America. New York: Baker & Taylor, 1911.

[ If ] I and my family were with you, we should not have been exposed
to the vengeance of our enemies, who rob us of the goods which God hath
given us to the sustinence of soule and body. I shall not assume to write
all the miseries that we suffer, which cannot be comprehended in a letter,
but in many books. I shall tell you briefly, that our temple is condemned,
and razed, our ministers banished forever, all their goods confiscated, and
moreover they are condemned to the fine of a thousand crowns. All the
other temples are also razed, except the temple of Re, and two or three
others. By act of Parliament we are hindered to be masters in any trade
or skill. We expect every day the lord governour or Guiene, whom shall
put soldiers in our houses, and take away our children to be offered to the
Idol, as they have done in the other countrys.

The country where you live [ New England ] is in great estime; I and a
grat many others, Protestants, intend to go there. Tell us, if you please,
what advantage we can have there, and particularly the boors who are ac-
customed to plow the ground. If somebody of your country would hazard to
come here with a ship to fetch in our French Protestants, he would make
great gain.

## THE HUGUENOTS IN SOUTH CAROLINA
### 1701

In 1701 John Lawson, an English traveler, published the following description of the Huguenot
settlements along the Santee River in A Journal
of a Thousand Miles Travelled Through Several
Nations of the Indians.

Source: Lucian J. Fosdick, The French Blood
in America. New York: Baker & Taylor Co.,
1911.

The first place we designed for was Santee River, where there is a
colony of French Protestants allowed and encouraged by the lords proprie-
tary. As we rowed up the river we found the land towards the mouth scarce
anything but a swamp, affording vast cypress trees of which the French
make canoes, that will carry fifty or sixty barrels. There being a strong
current in Santee River caused us to make but small way with our oars.
With hard rowing we got that night to Monsieur Eugee's [Huger's] house,
which stands about fifteen miles up the river, being the first Christian
dwelling we met with in that settlement, and were very courteously received by him and his wife. Many of the French follow a trade with the
Indians, living very conveniently for that interest. There are about seventy
families scattered on this river, who live as decently and happily as any
planters in these southward parts of America. The French being a temper-
ate, industrious people, some of them bringing very little of effects, yet by
their endeavors and mutual assistance among themselves, which is highly
to be commended, have outstripped our English, who brought with them
large fortunes, though, as it seems, less endeavour to manage their talent
to the best advantage.

## FRANCE ON THE OHIO
### 1749

During the mid-eighteenth century, French
exploration parties ventured south to the
Ohio Valley to establish firm claims to the
areas previously visited only sporadically.
These expeditions left a series of lead tab-
lets to mark French presence and the claims
of Louis XV. The following inscription was
translated from a tablet left by Pierre Joseph
de Céloron de Blainville near the Ohio River
in 1749.

Source: Ralph Henry Gabriel, The Pageant of
America. New Haven: Yale University Press,
1925. From Volume 6, "The Winning of Free-
dom" by Wood and Gabriel, copyright United
States Publishers Association, Inc.

In the year 1749, in the reign of Louis XV, King of France, We, Céloron, commandant of a detachment sent by the Marquis de la Galissoniere,
Commandant in Chief of New France, to re-establish peace in certain villages of the Indians of these districts, have buried this plate at the mouth
of the river Chinodahichetha, the eighteenth of August, near the Ohio, or
Beautiful river, as a monument of the renewal of the possession that we
have taken of the said river Ohio, of all its tributaries, and of all the lands
on both sides to the sources of the said rivers, as the preceding Kings of
France have enjoyed or sought to have enjoyed it, and which they have
maintained by force of arms and by treaties, especially by those of Ryswick,
Utrecht, and Aix-la-Chapelle.

ROCHAMBEAU'S INSTRUCTIONS
1780

>One of the primary reasons for tension between
>the allies, and for the failure of the Franco-
>American campaign in Rhode Island in 1778, was
>the lack of a united command.  The Comte
>d'Estaing did not trust American commanders
>enough to place his French regulars under their
>command, and the Americans refused to sub-
>ordinate themselves to French officers.  Louis
>XVI, and Vergennes, his minister of foreign
>affairs, displayed great insight and courage in
>solving this problem through the following orders,
>which Rochambeau was directed not to open until
>he was in the mid-Atlantic.

>Source:  Stephen Bonsal, When the French Were
>Here.  Garden City: Doubleday, Doran & Co.,
>Inc., 1945.

In sending this corps which His Majesty has furnished with its proper
complement of artillery for sieges and service in the field, in sending such
considerable succors to co-operate with General Washington, commander
in chief of the troops of the Congress of the United States of North America,
in the military operations which he may determine upon the intentions of
His Majesty are:

I.  That the General to whom His Majesty entrusts the command of his
troops should always and in all cases be under the command of General
Washington.

II.  That the projects and plans for the campaign, or for private expeditions, should be decided upon by the American General, keeping in view
the harmony which His Majesty hopes to see maintained between the two
commanders in chief as well as the generals and the soldiers of the two
nations.

III.  The French troops, being only auxiliaries, should, on this account,
as was done in Germany in the campaign of 1757, yield precedence and the
right to the American troops; and this decision is to hold good in all general
or particular cases which may occur.

IV.  In consequences of the above article the American officers with
equal rank and the same date of commission shall have the command, and
in all cases the American troops shall take the right.  In all military pro-
ceedings and capitulations the American General and Troops shall be named
first and will sign first, as has always been the custom, and in accordance
with the principles above laid down in regard to auxiliary troops.

V.  It is His Majesty's expectation and very positive order to Count de Rochambeau that he will see to the exact and literal execution of the above four Articles.

## AMERICAN ATTITUDES TOWARD ROCHAMBEAU'S ARMY
### 1781

Due in large part to religious differences and the
hostilities engendered by the long series of wars
between the French and English colonies in the
New World, Americans held a very low opinion
of Frenchmen. The regard that many Americans
had for Rochambeau's army is vividly illustrated
below by Abbé Claude Robin, a member of the
Regiment de Soissonais.

Source: Stephen Bonsal, When the French Were
Here. Garden City: Doubleday, Doran & Co.,
Inc., 1945.

Before the war the Americans regarded the French as enslaved to des-
potism, a prey to all manner of superstitions and prejudices; as people quite
incapable of solid and consistent effort, only occupied in such matters as
curling their hair and painting their faces, and far from being respecters
of the most sacred duties. These prejudices had been spread and empha-
sized by the English; then, at the beginning of the war, not a few things
happened to confirm these unfavorable opinions. The great majority of the
French who came to America when the rumor of revolution reached them
were men who had lost their reputations and were wholly in debt and who
generally presented themselves under false names and titles of nobility to
which they had no manner of right. Under these false pretenses some of
them obtained high rank in the American Army, also considerable advances
in money, and then disappeared. The simplicity of the Americans and their
lack of world experience made tricks of this nature very easy.

These prejudices were in full control when Rochambeau arrived and
we all saw the extreme importance of dissipating them. High officers established the most strict discipline and the others were careful to exhibit
that politeness and amenity which has always characterized the French nobility. Even our common soldiers became mild, careful, and moderate,
and in the course of our long sojourn not a single complaint was brought
against them. Our young nobles who, because of their birth and fortune
and their residence at court, should have been most attached to dissipation,
to luxury, and all the appareils de la grandeur, were the very first to give
an example of complete simplicity and to accept the requirements of the
frugal life. They always showed themselves most affable to their new neigh-
bors, quite as though they had never come in contact with any other kind of
men; and when this line of conduct had been maintained for a few weeks a
complete revolution in the spirit of the people was noticed. Even the Tories
and Royalists could not help loving the French.

ROCHAMBEAU MEETS A CONNECTICUT REPUBLICAN
1781

> There are, of course, many anecdotes that
> may be told regarding the French presence
> in America during the Revolution. The fol-
> lowing incident was related by the Comte de
> Rochambeau in his memoirs.

> Source: Memoirs of the Marshall Count De
> Rochambeau. New York: The New York Times
> and Arno Press, 1971.

The conveyance in which I proceeded to the conference, in company
with Admiral de Ternay, who, by the way, was very infirm, broke down.
I dispatched my first aide-de-camp, Fersen, to fetch a wheelwright, who
lived about a mile from the spot where the accident occurred. He soon after
returned to us, however, and informed us that he had found the man sick
with the ague, and that he had positively declared to him that for his hat
full of guineas he would do no work at night. I prevailed on the admiral
to accompany me to the man's shop, and we repaired thither; we told him
that General Washington would arrive at Hartford that same evening, to
confer with us the following day, and that unless he could repair our carriage, we should be too late to meet him. "You are no liars, at any rate,"
he replied; "for I read in the Connecticut paper that Washington was to be
there to confer with you; as it is for the public service I will take care that
your carriage shall be ready for you at six in the morning." He kept his
word; and we proceeded on at the promised time. As we returned, another
wheel broke, and we were once more obliged to have recourse to our old
friend. "Well!" said he, "so you want me to work again for you at night?"
"Aye! indeed, we do," I replied: "Admiral Rodney has arrived to reinforce
threefold the naval forces against which we are contending and it is of the
highest importance that we should return without delay to Rhode Island to
oppose him." "But what can you do," he continued, "with your six ships
against the twenty English?" "It will be the most glorious day of our life
if they attempt to break our line." "Come, come," said he, "you are good
honest fellows; your carriage shall be put in repair by to-morrow morning
at five o'clock. But tell me, before I set to work, although I do not wish to
inquire into your secrets, how did you like Washington, and how did he like
you?" We assured him that we had been delighted with him; his patriotism
was satisfied, and he kept his word. I do not mean to compare all Americans to this good man; but almost all the inland cultivators and all the land
owners of Connecticut are animated with that patriotic spirit, which many
other people would do well to imitate.

## THE CASTORLAND COMPANY
### 1793

During the period of the French Revolution
and the Napoleonic Wars many refugee colonies were established in the United States by
both Royalists and Republicans. The following document is the prospectus of the "New
York Company," generally known as the Castorland Company, whose constitution was
signed in Paris, June 28, 1793.

The original document is in the State Museum,
Albany, New York.

Several individuals attracted by a consideration of the interior and sur-
rounding advantages of the extensive and valuable domains to which their
attention has been drawn, have devised the means for developing these resources and of offering the speculation to Europeans.

They have observed that this tract offers in its fertility all the riches
of agriculture in the fine distribution of its waters, the conveniences of an
extended commerce, and in its location in the immediate vicinity of a population wealthy by their own capital, and all the benefits of Liberty with ex-
emption from all subsidies.

These incontestable facts are obtained without artifice, and proved by
the mere inspection of the geography of New York, and from the general
acquaintance we have concerning that State.

But they have felt that the value of this vast estate might be enhanced
in the activity of cultivation and settlement if the proprietors were to become mutually interested in their own labors; and that they might become
in some way as one family, united by common interests and common wants,
by which they would hasten the general success by combining from the beginning the various relations of their association.

To maintain this essential unity of interests these persons have devised
a plan that shall make each of the associates specially interested in the
whole of the property, and they have accordingly required that a division
shall be made by lot, giving to each one at once fifty acres, leaving fifty
more in the portion that is to remain their common property until a fixed
period. To enable these subdivisions to be made in an easy and economi-
cal way, they have adopted a form of stock certificate...as combining these
desireable ends in the best manner, and as possessing the advantage of as-
suring the first title of purchase, and the remaining fractions, and of par-
taking of the nature of an authentic title.

They have therefore secured the purchase, and have agreed that it shall be made in the name of Sieur Chassanis, upon whom they have united their confidence, with the duty of signing the certificates of stock and as the funds were paid in to remit them to each one as his title to the property, or he will furnish declarations to such as may prefer it.

Subsequent to this contract, the parties interested, have established the following basis, which shall be the Common Law of the stock holders and inseparable from the resulting title.

This regulation is divided into two parts, the first embracing the features essential to the title, and the immutable law of the purchasers. The other includes the regulations for guiding their common interests.

## Part First

Article I. The six hundred thousand acres of land which Sieur Chassanis has bought of William Constable, including in addition five acres gratuitous to each hundred, shall be subdivided into six thousand shares, which number is to be the precise number of subdivisions.

Art. II. The holder of stock may make himself known as such when he wishes, and receive the title directly in his own name.

Art. III. The certificates of stock shall be all on one model, and as follows: -- "Title of Association of the New York Company in the purchase of six hundred thousand acres of land, located in Montgomery County, State of New York. The holder of this certificate, having paid the sum of eight hundred livres, is made a Proprietor of one hundred acres in a tract of six hundred thousand acres of land, which has been conveyed to me, as representing the Company of stock holders, according to an agreement of this date, which requires me to pass all requisite title for this portion of the property, in favor of the holder of this certificate, whenever he may wish to own title in his own name. The present certificate is for an integral part, and a remaining fraction of the purchase above given, by virtue of which the holder shall participate in all the rights of this association whereof the foundation and regulation are established by the fundamental articles annexed to the common title. This certificate bears the number . . . .; In faith of which, it has been signed by me, countersigned by the Commissaries of the Company and inspected by M. Lambot, Notary, in Paris, this . . . ."

These certificates shall be deposited in the hands of M. Lambot, Notary at Paris, who shall attend to their issue, after being properly signed and inspected as hereinafter mentioned.

The price of the shares shall remain fixed at 800 livres, which shall be paid into the hands of the said M. Lambot.

Of this sum, one tenth part shall be placed at the disposal of the Commissaries to be by them used in the expenses of the establishment, such as, providing utensils, materials, and provisions, in opening roads, and the necessary constructions, surveys, and development.

The remaining nine tenths shall belong to the vendor, and shall be re-mitted to him after the titles, by which the said Sieur Constable is to transfer this property, shall be returned from America, executed in all the formalities required by the customs of the country.

This remittance shall be made by Depository, the received being forwarded to Messrs Ransom Moreland and Hammersley, Bankers in London, by drafts upon that city. This remittance shall be made from time to time as it is received, without waiting for the return of the titles; but until such return the said Sieur William Constable shall not draw these funds from the hands of the said London Bankers.

Art. V. The six hundred thousand acres shall be subdivided into twelve thousand lots of fifty acres each, of which six thousand shall be set apart and drawn at the beginning, as private property. The remaining six thousand shall belong to the Society, who shall take subsequent measures to give it value, and of which the distribution is hereinafter regulated.

Art. VI. Each shareholder shall have a right to one of these divided lots, and an interest in another lot of the undivided tract.

Art. VII. The thirty thousand acres resulting from the surplus of measure shall be used as follows, namely:

Two thousand in the formation of a city in the interior of the tract, upon the banks of the great river that flows through the Concession. Two thousand acres more for the formation of another city upon the shores of Lake Ontario, at the mouth of the river upon which the other city is built, to serve as a port and entrepôt of Commerce.

Six thousand shall be assigned to the artisans who may be scattered through the country, such as potters, carpenters, locksmiths, joiners, &ct., to be charged to them after seven years, at a rent of twelve sous per acre.

And the twenty thousand acres left, shall be used for the construction of roads and bridges, or otherwise used by the society.

Art. 8. The locations of the two cities shall be divided into fourteen thousand lots, of which two thousand shall be reserved for markets, -- edifices, such as Churches Schools and other public institutions, and for poor artisans who may wish to settle there. The remaining twelve thousand lots shall form two classes, of which one shall be divided and the other remain undivided, and one lot of each class shall belong to each holder of a share of stock.

Art 9. The choice of the divided lots, as well of lands, as in the cities, shall belong to the holders of Shares in the order of the date of presentation of their titles, by themselves, or their attorney's to the Commissaries of the Company.

Art. X. The Commissaries of the Company upon the tract, at the end of Seven Years, shall make a report upon the property remaining in common, its character, and the improvements of which it is susceptable, with an estimate of its value.

After this report, there shall be a division into six thousand lots, which shall be designated upon a map. The shareholders shall be notified three months previously to the drawing which shall take place in a general assembly, for only who shall have given notice fifteen days beforehand, that they wish to receive their share at that time.

Those who may not have given this notice, shall be deemed to have elected to continue without division, and under a common régime.

Art. XI. The shareholders who may still remain in the society shall in general Assembly regulate their particular interests, as well for the administration of the remaining land, as for their Sale according as they may determine.

Art. XII. After this drawing, the society shall no longer exist, except as among those shareholders who have not preferred to participate in the lots. The shares drawn shall be certified to the bearers by an extract of the record of the drawing and adjudication upon their lots.

Art. XIII. The interests of the Company shall be regulated by Commissaries residing in Paris, three in number, and by at least two others living upon the tract. These several Commissaries shall be in habitual Correspondence, and shall be nominated by an absolute majority of the General Assembly. These Assemblies shall be held in Paris, and every shareholder shall there be counted by shares; but no single person shall however count for more than five votes, whatever may be the number or shares he represents.

Art. XIV. All the above articles are essential to the origin of the shares, and can only be modified by a general Assembly convened ad hoc, and by a majority of two thirds.

## Part Second
### Regime

Article I. Within one month, there shall be held a general Assembly of the subscribers at the rooms of the said Sieur Chassannis, No. 20, Rue de la Gussienne, Paris, for the purpose of nominating Commissaries.

Art. II. The Commissaries residing in Paris shall be charged with the duty of proving the shares in the hands of the Depository, and or putting upon each one of them the certificate of inspection to the end of guaranteeing still further against errors of every kind. The Notary with whom they are deposited, shall also add his certificate according as their price is received, and they shall furthermore be signed by the said Sieur Chassannis, for delivery to the shareholders.

There shall therefore be issued no certificates of stock until after the execution of these inspections and signatures, and the subscribers in the mean time shall receive only a provisional receipt from the Depository.

Art. III. To prevent the least error in distribution, the Certificates of Stock, shall be registered by numbers, by the Sieur Chassannis, upon their delivery to the holders, at his office, and without this registration of which mention shall be endorsed upon the Certificate by the said Sieur Chassannis, and by the person whom the Commissaries shall appoint for this purpose.

No shareholder shall be admitted to the Assembly, none have the right to present the date for his choice of location.

Art. IV. The Commissaries nominated for going to America, shall be bearers of the Instructions and general Powers of the Assembly, and shall there survey the tract, locate the sites of the two cities, and prepare upon the spot, for the Society, within three months after their arrival, a report of their verifications and labors, with a detailed map of the common property.

Art. V. These Commissaries shall be chosen from among the Stockholders.

Art. VI. They shall decide upon the location of the fifty acre lots to be originally distributed to each share of stock, after which the Selections of the Shareholders shall be made.

Art. VII. The locations shall be verified upon two registers, in the charge of the Commissaries in America, one of which they shall send annually to the General Assembly in France.

Art. VIII. The direct titles for delivery to those Share holders as may wish to be thus known, shall consist of a Declaration by Sieur Chassannis, that within his general purchase, there belongs such a portion . . . . to enjoy conformably with the common title and the Social Compact thereunto annexed. This Declaration shall be numbered to correspond with the Certificate which shall remain thereunto annexed, under pain of forfeiture of the Declaration; always further providing that the Certificate shall be cancelled previously. This title shall not be complete until after its registration by the Commissaries, which they shall do upon presentation.

Art. IX. The Commissaries in America shall be clothed with Special power by Sieur Chassons, to confer like titles upon those who may require it. This power should be given at the foot of a blank form of the Declaration, with the view of maintaining uniformity of entry.

Art. X. The deliberations and acts of the Company done in France, do not require as for the Commissaries, any public formality, when they are legalized by the minister or other public functionary of the United States resident in France.

Art. XI. There shall be delivered upon demand, a duplicate of the title to any holders of Stock, which shall resemble the originals, but shall make mention therein of the delivery of such duplicates.

## TALLEYRAND AND THE XYZ AFFAIR
### 1798

In 1798 American feelings toward France were
strained by the report that French negotiators
identified only as "X, Y, and Z" had suggested
the United States pay them a bribe to speed negotiations. In the following letter penned by
Talleyrand to Elbridge Gerry, the French Minister indicated he had no knowledge of, and did
not condone, the suggestions made by the mysterious X, Y and Z.

Source: Ralph Henry Gabriel, The Pageant of
America. New Haven: Yale University Press,
1925. From Volume 8, "Builders of the Republic" by Ogg, copyright United States Publishers
Association, Inc.

The Minister of Foreign Affairs
   to Mr. Gerry, Envoy of the United States.
   I have received, Sir, your letter of yesterday. You inform me, 1st,
that the journal presented contains all the informal negotiations communi-
cated by the envoys to their government; 2nd, that the persons in question
have not produced to your knowledge any authorization or document of any
kind that would accredit them; 3rd, that three of the individuals mentioned
(designating them in the order in which I have placed them as W, X, Y.)
are foreigners, and that the fourth, or Z, has acted only as messenger
and interpreter.
   Although I understand your reluctance to name these individuals, I
must beg you at once to subordinate this to the importance of the matter.
Will you please therefore, 1st, either give me their names in writing, or
tell them confidentially to the bearer; 2nd, name the woman referred to by
Mr. Pinckney; 3rd, tell me whether any of the citizens attached to my staff
and authorized by me to see the envoys have said one word which has the
least relation to the shocking proposal that has been made by X and Y to
remit any sum whatever for corrupt distribution.
                              Talleyrand

## SPAIN CEDES LOUISIANA TO FRANCE
### 1802

In 1802 Joseph Napoleon, king of Spain, deeded
Louisiana to France. Though the whole territory would be sold to the United States in a few
weeks, the proclamation issued announcing the
transfer to France left a different impression
entirely. The proclamation was not issued in
Louisiana until November 30, 1803.

Source: Ralph Henry Gabriel, The Pageant of
America. New Haven, Yale University Press,
1925. From Volume 8, "Builders of the Republic" by Ogg, copyright United States Publishers
Association, Inc.

In the name of the French Republic, Victor, General of Division, Captain General of Louisiana, to the Louisianians.

Dear Louisianians:

By a treaty made between the French Government and His Majesty the
King of Spain, Louisiana has become the property of the French Republic.
I come in the name of its First Consul, the immortal Napoleon, to take possession of your interesting Colony, and to join your fortunes to the brilliant
destinies of the French People.

Up to the present time, dear Louisianians, in spite of your wise conduct, and all your efforts for the aggrandizement of your Colony, you have
been able to stamp the result of your activities only within the narrow circle
of your old possessions; you have not been able to take advantage of all the
resources offered for agriculture in this vast and fecund territory; you have
not been able to turn to the profit of a larger commerce all the rich fruits
of your happy soil.

I come in the name of our Government to offer you means to multiply
your pleasures; I bring you the laws that have made the glory of the French
Nation, for they assure its tranquillity and its happiness. Surrounded by
just and enlightened magistrates, we shall vie with you in establishing in-
corruptible justice in your midst. A wise and far-sighted administration
will give movement and life to agriculture and to all branches of industry
and commerce. I bring you brothers like myself who even though we have
not previously met you, know you well enough to esteem and cherish you.
Henceforth all delightfully mingling together, we shall form a family, each
one of whose members shall work for the happiness and prosperity of all.

I shall feel for you the tenderness of the father that I have become; I shall show unceasingly the solicitude of the mother-country to provide the Colony with anything that it may need.

Dear Louisianians, do not fear the imposing group of warriors who surround me. The glory that they have acquired in battle merits your esteem; the virtues that distinguish them will permit you to love them. They shall respect your rights and your properties, and I assure you that you can only praise their conduct. As for myself, dear Louisianians, my happiness will be assured if I can assure your own by my watchfulness and my care.

Victor

## AN APPEAL TO THE LOUISIANA FRENCH
### 1815

When the British assault on New Orleans was
imminent in 1814-15, troops were needed for
the defense of the city. French-born residents
were technically not required to bear arms for
the United States government, but Brig. Gen.
Jean Joseph Amable Humbert rallied them to the
cause with the following appeal.

Source: Simone de la Souchere Deléry, Napoleon's
Soldiers in America. Gretna: Pelican Publishing
Co., 1972.

Frenchmen,

You will arm yourselves to defend a country who granted you a refuge
when British intrigues had left you homeless. You will be fighting for people who have welcomed you as brothers and given you the right of citizens.
Honor, patriotism, gratitude urge you to fight and I do hope this appeal
will find you responsive.

Humbert, Brigadier General

## THE FRENCH IN CALIFORNIA
### 1849

> Among those "Forty-Niners" who rushed to the
> California gold fields were literally thousands
> of French immigrants.  The following is an ex-
> cerpt from a description detailing some of the
> problems that a French traveler named Montes
> Jean encountered around San Francisco in De-
> cember, 1849.

> Reproduced with permission of the publisher
> from French Activities in California, by
> Abraham P. Nasatir (Stanford:  Stanford Uni-
> versity Press, 1945) pp. 393-4.

My dear father:

It is twenty-four days since we arrived in California, but in what condition; abandoned by the management and by each one of the associes tra-
vailleurs.  All of us were landed without M. Lannois, son of the armateur,
having given us supplies for even twenty-four hours, distributing to us only
our tents.  It was only the great threats which we made that forced them to
give them to us.  The courage which has never failed us has not yet left us.
We have been very fortunate being in a country where a great deal is earned
and where work is not lacking.  I say "work"; that is to say, go to the dock
of San Francisco, become a working man, carry bales of merchandise to
various stores and you will be quite well paid.  For carrying a trunk weigh-
ing about a hundred livres for a distance of fifty meters or more one is paid
three dollars (about sixteen francs); and in this way we have lived up to now,
when I am writing you.  But at present, since people are arriving in large
numbers, prices are diminishing greatly.  One cannot go to the mines at
this time on account of the rising waters and because the routes are miry
and submerged.  Next March we intend, six of us who are living together,
to leave for the placers, which are sixty or eighty leagues from San Francisco.  Bache is one of the six of us who are together.  Fevers are the principal ills of the country; but up to the present none of us have had anything
about which to complain.  Not one of us six has been attacked by this mal-
ady.

Food is very expensive in this country.  Bread, for example, costs a
half-dollar a livre, and meat twenty-six sous de France.  Work is not pro-
gressing very much at present, although there are two hundred vessels in
the harbor.  Yesterday we spent the day at a fire which consumed one-third
of the city of San Francisco.  The alcalde is very pleased with the French,

who distinguished themselves on this occasion, although there were two who were victims of their self-denial. Powder, which is cheap enough in the country, has served to make many more ravages. We were going to work at demolishing a house, when at a distance of from ten to fifteen meters an explosion of three or four hundred <u>livres</u> of powder made the materials fly into pieces more than fifty meters in the air, and woe to those who were not lively enough to avoid them.

"FRENCH POWER" IN AMERICA
1949

Beginning in the 1950s a popular movement for
the study and recognition of ethnic heritage
swept the United States. While it concentrated
primarily on the more "visible" minorities in
American society -- blacks, Chicanos and Indians -- there were many who spoke out on behalf of French contributions to American heritage. The following document is a letter written to the editor of The Saturday Review by
Timothy G. Turner in September, 1949.

Allan Nevins overstates his case in reviewing "Our English Heritage"
by Gerald W. Johnson. It is but another case, all too common in recent
years, of ignoring the influence of French thought in the Americas.

Mr. Nevins says "our culture is as distinctly an Anglo-American culture as that of Quebec is Franco-American." He says our "fundamental
political concepts are primarily of British origin." This is only looking at
surfaces. There was something unique, in both the Americas, which set
up the American republics.

The American revolution would never have happened had it not been for
French thought. Montesquieu, Rousseau, and Voltaire were read and re-
read by the founding fathers. Montesquieu, it is true, noted the good things
in the English political system, which the English themselves did not real-
ize. But his evaluation of them was French.

Something happened in this country that could never have happened in
a country dominated by British ideas, for the British -- despite their ideas
of personal liberty -- are monarchists to the core. The most radical and
astonishing thing happened in the thirteen colonies at the end of the eighteenth
century. A secular government based on the sovereignty of the people was
set up. The only Englishman who seems to have been carried away by the
French radical thought that made this possible was Thomas Paine.

I cannot speak for the French-Canadians, but I know the Latin Americans pretty well. I can assure Messrs. Johnson and Nevins that their revo-
lutions early in the nineteenth century were similarly dominated by the intellectual ideas that swept through the educated classes at that period in
history. The Latin American republics were modeled after the republics
set up in the United States and in France. Spanish thought had no effect.
It was French thought plus an independency that seems to have resulted
from pioneering life in the whole of the Western Hemisphere.

The English to this day do not understand the spirit of the American
Revolution for the reason, perhaps, that French thought never dented their

intellectual isolation. I can understand this. But I cannot understand why so many American scholars ignore the influence of French eighteenth-century thought in the making of their own country.

## CHARLES DE GAULLE ON CANADA
1967

While French-American relations were strained
by the policy of the French government under the
leadership of Charles de Gaulle, sentiments in
the United States did not reach the fever propor-
tions that they did in Canada following de Gaulle's
visit to Québec Province in July, 1967. The following excerpt of one of his speeches, as recorded
by the New York Times, indicates what many Canadians believed was his blatant attempt to rouse
support for the Front de libération du Québec,
which had been founded in 1963. His closing re-
marks, "Vive le Québec libre!," only served to
heighten their fears.

Source:© 1967 by the New York Times Company. Reprinted by permission.

Refusing to be subject any longer to the prevalence of influences alien
to you in the fields of thought, culture and science, you must have your
own elites, universities, laboratories. Far from playing second fiddle as
in the past in your own progress, you are determined to create and direct
it and to get therefore the necessary teachers, administrators, engineers,
technicians and specialists.

Instead of letting outside concerns put to use your territory's vast resources, you intend yourselves to discover, organize and exploit them.
. . . .

What the French over here, once they are their own masters, will have
to do in concert with the other Canadians is to organize ways and means
for safeguarding their essence and independence next to the colossal state
which is their neighbor.

BIBLIOGRAPHY


Baird, Charles W., History of the Huguenot Emigration to America. New
    York, 1885.

Balch, Thomas, The French in America During the War of Independence
    of the United States, 1777-1783. Boston: Gregg Press, 1972.

Beers, Henry P., The French in North America; a Bibliographical Guide
    to French Archives, Reproductions, and Research Missions. Baton
    Rouge: Louisiana State University Press, 1957.

Bond, Beverly W., Jr., The Monroe Mission to France, 1794-1796. Balti-
    more: Johns Hopkins Press, 1907.

Bonsal, Stephen, When the French Were Here. Garden City: Doubleday,
    Doran and Co., 1945.

Charlevoix, Pierre François Xavier de, History of New France. New York,
    1868.

Childs, Frances S., French Refugee Life in the United States, 1790-1800.
    Baltimore: Johns Hopkins University Press, 1940.

Clarke, T. Wood, Émigrés in the Wilderness. New York: Kennikat Press,
    1941.

Corwin, Edward S., French Policy and the American Alliance of 1778.
    Princeton, 1916.

Davie, Maurice, Refugees in America. 1947.

Deléry, Simone de la Souchère, Napoleon's Soldiers in America. Gretna:
    Pelican Publishing Co., 1972.

Eccles, William J., France in America. New York: Harper & Row, 1972.

Fecteau, Edward, French Contributions to America. Methven, Mass.:
    Soucy Press, 1945.

Fosdick, Lucian J., The French Blood in America. New York: Baker and Taylor, 1911.

Gayarré, Charles E.A., History of Louisiana; the French Domination. New York, 1867, and New Orleans, 1903.

Hirsch, Arthur H., The Huguenots of Colonial South Carolina. 1928.

Hughes, Thomas A., History of the Society of Jesus in North America. New York, 1907-1917.

Jones, Howard M., America and French Culture, 1750-1848. Chapel Hill: University of North Carolina Press, 1927.

Kunz, Virginia B., The French in America. Minneapolis: Lerner Publications, 1966.

Lindsay, J.T., French Exiles in Louisiana. New York: W.B. Smith & Co., 1881.

Monaghan, Frank, French Travellers in the United States, 1765-1932. New York: 1933.

Murray, Elsie, Azilum, French Refugee Colony of 1793. Athens, Pa.: Tioga Point Museum, 1940.

Nasatir, Abraham P., French Activities in California: An Archival Calendar Guide. Stanford: Stanford University Press, 1945.

Perkins, James B., France in the American Revolution. Williamstown, Mass.: Corner House Publishers, 1970.

Roncière, Charles de la, What the French Have Done in America. Paris: Typographie Plon-Nourrit et Cie, 1915.

Rosengarten, Joseph G., French Colonists and Exiles in the United States. Philadelphia: J.B. Lippincott, 1907.

Saxon, Lyle, Lafitte the Pirate. New Orleans: Robert L. Crager & Co., 1930.

Thwaites, Reuben G., France in America, 1497-1763. New York: 1905.

Zoltvany, Yves F., The French Tradition in America. Columbia: University of South Carolina Press, 1969.

## SELECTED INDEX OF IMPORTANT FRENCH NAMES

The following list includes, due to space limitation, only the more important French names that appear in the chronology section of this book. The reader is urged to consult dates or time periods for additional names and information.